Praise for my Concours Group colleagues-Tom Casey, T[...]

Tom Casey and his collaborators have captured nicely the emergi[...]
tives. "At the end of the day it is all about the people". The ex[...]
Concours Group, led to the inevitable conclusion that the Human [...]
*it **Talent Readiness** is an essential variable for enterprise success and without it failure is inevitable.*

Ron Christman PhD, Former Chairman and Chief Executive Officer

The Concours Group

*Tom Casey and **his collaborators,** Tim Donahue and Eric Seubert are spot on with their assertion*
that the human equation drives enterprise success. As a senior executive of a diversified highly spe-
*cialized global company I can attest that the issue of **Talent Readiness** is a front of mind concern.*
The insights the authors have captured are exceptional.

Laurent Potdevin, Former CEO

Burton Snowboards

*TJX has worked closely with Tom Casey and **Discussion Partner Collaborative** on Human*
Capital Transformation efforts. As the senior HR officer of a global organization with tens of
*thousands employees the concept of **Talent Readiness** is of paramount importantce to all of us*
chartered to lead the HR efforts or our companies. Candidly a lack of attention to shifting demo-
graphics and employee engagement challenges lacks foresight.

Greg Flores, Chief Human Resources Officer

The TJX Companies

*As the CIO of a global organization I highly endorse the concept of **Talent Readiness** promoted*
by Tom Casey and his contributors. The IT space is highly dynamic with shifting demands from
stakeholders and an ever evolving need for added capabilities of our professionals. In point of fact,
IT is one of the most fluid domains in an enterprise. The role of the CIO, as presented in this book,
is to stay ahead of the curve in understanding the labor market and drivers of employee engagement.

Ina Kamenz, Chief Information Officer

Thermo Fisher Scientific

TALENT READINESS

THE FUTURE IS NOW

TALENT READINESS

THE FUTURE IS NOW

Leading a
Multi-Generational Workforce

*With the **right** people*

*...in the **right** place*

*...at the **right** time*

*...with the **right** motivation*

BY
TOM CASEY
WITH TIM DONAHUE AND ERIC SEUBERT

Published by Advantage, Charleston, South Carolina.
Member of Advantage Media Group.

ADVANTAGE is a registered trademark and the Advantage colophon is a trademark of Advantage Media Group, Inc.

Printed in the United States of America.

ISBN: 978-1-59932-221-6
LCCN: 2010913765

This publication is designed to provide accurate and authoritative information in regard to the subject matter covered. It is sold with the understanding that the publisher is not engaged in rendering legal, accounting, or other professional services. If legal advice or other expert assistance is required, the services of a competent professional person should be sought.

Advantage Media Group is proud to be a part of the Tree Neutral™ program. Tree Neutral offsets the number of trees consumed in the production and printing of this book by taking proactive steps such as planting trees in direct proportion to the number of trees used to print books. To learn more about Tree Neutral, please visit www.treeneutral.com. To learn more about Advantage's commitment to being a responsible steward of the environment, please visit www.advantagefamily.com/green

Advantage Media Group is a leading publisher of business, motivation, and self-help authors. Do you have a manuscript or book idea that you would like to have considered for publication? Please visit www.amgbook.com or call 1.866.775.1696

Acknowledgements

*"My appreciation to all the C's in my life nuclear
and extended, also of course the Renners."*

-Tom Casey

*"My deep gratitude to Cathy for her enduring
encouragement and support."*

-Tim Donahue

*Mom and Dad. Thank you for giving me a solid foundation.
It has been easier building my adult life than what it
could have been, and frequently is, for many others.*

*Virginia. Eighteen years ago, no one could have predicted
the journey we were about to take. I am very blessed that you
accepted my invitation on Christmas Eve and forever grateful
that you stayed with me "through good times and in bad."*

*God. Thank you for everything. It is true,
through You, all things are possible.*

-Eric Seubert

ABOUT DISCUSSION PARTNER COLLABORATIVE

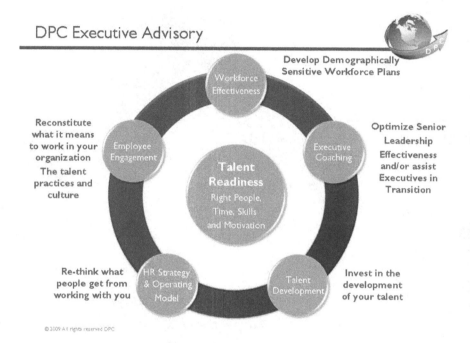

DPC Executive Advisory

Develop Demographically
Sensitive Workforce Plans

Workforce
Effectiveness

Reconstitute
what it means
to work in your
organization
The talent
practices and
culture

Employee
Engagement

Talent
Readiness
Right People,
Time, Skills
and Motivation

Executive
Coaching

Optimize Senior
Leadership
Effectiveness
and/or assist
Executives in
Transition

Re-think what
people get from
working with you

HR Strategy
& Operating
Model

Talent
Development

Invest in the
development
of your talent

Discussion Partner Collaborative is a global research driven executive advisory providing Talent Readiness services to C-suite executives. **DPC's** network includes more than 200 consultants in nineteen locations around the world. Clients range from Fortune 100 businesses to start-ups. **www.discussionpartners.com**

TABLE OF CONTENTS

INTRODUCTION

What Concerns the Informed Leader

It was a storm beyond imagining. As Hurricane Grace howled up the Atlantic Coast, two other weather fronts advanced from the north and west on a collision course. Buffeted at the focal point off the Massachusetts coast was the ill-fated Andrea Gail, gone fishing at a most inauspicious time.

"You could be a meteorologist all your life and never see something like this phenomenon. It would be a disaster of epic proportions. It would be... *The Perfect Storm*," the weatherman warns in the popular movie of that name, based on the best-seller by Sebastian Junger.

It's not hundred-foot waves that are thrashing the executive suite these days. Yet corporate leaders well might feel that way, for a confluence of challenging realities.

Another kind of storm threatens organizations worldwide venturing out from the global recession to go fishing again on rough waters. Unless they prove themselves far more seaworthy than the Andrea Gail, the storm could send them foundering into the deep.

A "PERFECT STORM" OF TALENT READINESS

In their book "Workforce Crisis," authors Ken Dychtwald, Tamara Erickson and Robert Morison describe the brewing storm of human capital. Birth rates in the industrialized world have declined worldwide, and life spans have increased. As Baby Boomers prepare to retire in huge numbers, an already competitive labor market is seeing a growing imbalance between talent needs and talent availability.

Enlightened leaders recognize that they need to be more inventive in meeting these challenges in this era of global enterprise. As economic opportunities rebound, they need to embrace a new employee engagement approach if they are to move forward decisively into a bright future. They understand that they must institute a new workforce strategy even before the problems are apparent to the organization as a whole.

As captains of their vessels, chief executive officers must help to navigate through the storm. It is a perfect one, indeed, whipped by these elemental forces:

- Lingering effects of the global recession

- Renewal of growth opportunities globally

- Aging of the global workforce and shifting demographics

- Decline in employee engagement and commitment

- Shortage of workers with critical skills

- Inefficient, ineffective talent management strategies

Today's workforce has changed dramatically, not only in ethnic, racial and gender terms, but also in terms of age. Aging populations and workforces are a global trend. This shift is so striking that it calls into question whether the prevailing approaches to human capital management could possibly be effective today.

As you can see in 2000 we were a fairly your world with a small percentage of the population above the age of 60. By contrast, 2025 our global population will have rapidly aged.

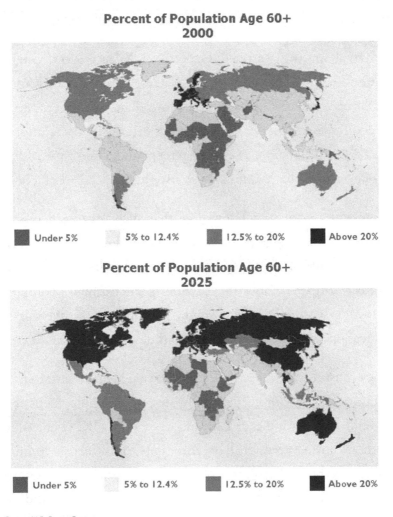

Percent of Population Age 60+
2000

Under 5%   5% to 12.4%   12.5% to 20%   Above 20%

Percent of Population Age 60+
2025

Under 5%   5% to 12.4%   12.5% to 20%   Above 20%

Source: U.S. Census Bureau

Corporate managers now find themselves dealing simultaneously with four generations of employees, from entry level through middle careerists to mature workers. Each generation has widely different expectations about the nature and conditions of employment. Ten years ago, companies were hiring Generation X workers for their entry-level positions. Now, the dominant generation at the entry level is Generation Y or Millennials and those workers bring with them different beliefs and behaviors that are creating challenges for today's managers. Their aspirations and the nature of their commitment are substantively different from those of their older colleagues.

What about the seasoned Generation X employees, ostensibly the future leaders, the ones with the highest potential to advance the organization? In recessionary times, more than ever was expected of those dedicated employees, yet career opportunities, recognition, and rewards suffered. Their level of engagement and commitment slipped. To help overcome that requires innovative human capital practices.

Companies need to acknowledge that such shifting demographics and declining engagement, well underway long before the global recession, require a new way of planning for the worker and the workforce. Organizations are becoming increasingly complex as they position themselves for growth, and they must likewise show sophistication and discipline in their staff development.

They must recognize, as well, that they are facing a severe shortage of certain workers with critical skills, despite unemployment reports that would seem to indicate a sizable labor pool. The talent shortfall threatens the hiring needs of all organizations – information technology specialists and trained project managers for example – and the specific needs of a variety of economic sectors such as oil, utilities and health care. Companies must work even harder to recruit, train and retain those employees who will meet their needs both for vital functions and future leadership.

Many executives have seen the storm clouds building. They are becoming aware of what they must do, even as they grapple with how best to do it.

Around the world, top executives face this paramount challenge: How do you get the right people in the right positions at the right time with the right skills and right motivations? They are ready to pursue the means of getting it right – and that requires leadership, innovation and creative human capital planning.

They are ready to pursue the goal of Talent Readiness.

EMERGING CONCERNS FROM THE C-SUITE

In this new climate of global enterprise in which businesses have been tempered by economic crisis and encouraged by a world of opportunity, we at **Discussion Partner Collaborative** have been hearing many of the same kind of questions arising from the C-suite:

1. What am I missing due to my being heads-down to address the recession?

2. Do I have the right people to get me through this crisis?

3. After the crisis, what type of managerial skills should my executives possess?

4. How should I plan for shifting demographics?

5. How can we use social networking to improve the engagement of our employees?

6. How can we leverage social networking to promote our employer brand and attract the best people?

7. Do I have the right skills to be a CEO?

8. How do I address the fact that enterprise engagement has declined?

In our executive advisory work, we are finding that our CEO and C-suite clients are focusing less on recessionary pressures and issues of restructuring, stock prices and governance. Discussions have shifted to issues of growth and globalization, so clearly related.

The common theme among all executives with whom we have been working is that the economic crisis changed business fundamentals. When they ask what they are missing, then, our answer has become: "It is hard to say. We are all navigating as-yet-unchartered waters." In such an environment, the following questions arise regarding strategy:

1. How do we focus our growth efforts domestically and outside our host country?

2. How do we manage a truly global workforce?

3. Given the frequent parochialism of Americans, how do we promote a sense of global enterprise community?

4. What is a reasonable return on investment in the context of forecasted turbulent stock market conditions?

5. Will the ultimate SEC measurement of intangibles be a benefit to our enterprise?

Using filters such as those five, C-suite managers have become highly reflective as they ponder their next steps. By considering the above, as we have learned from our client work, it is imperative that companies creatively improvise new strategies for managing their workforces.

AN IMPERATIVE FOR GROWTH

Managing human capital is a primary real-time challenge for senior leaders. A few key trends help to demonstrate the urgency. The following graph, for example, illustrates the dramatic age shift taking place in the composition of the domestic workforce.

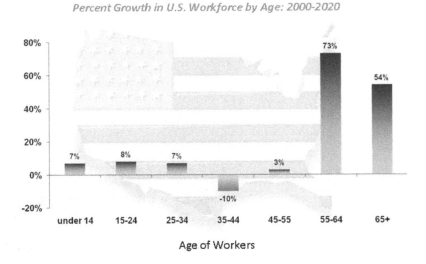

Percent Growth in U.S. Workforce by Age: 2000-2020

Source: U.S. Census Bureau

In a further complication, the domestic U.S. workforce is experiencing a post-graduate exodus of international students. Historically, students came to U.S. colleges such as the Massachusetts Institute of Technology because of the quality of the education and because they wanted to initially live and work in the United States. Today, a large percentage of foreign graduates are returning to their home countries to work, leaving an additional shortfall in qualified talent.

The dramatic decline in the growth of the working-age population in the United States is mirrored globally. Consider the statistics in the following graph.

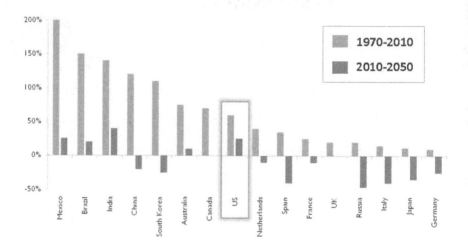

Source: Deloitte Research/UN Population Division (http://esa.un.org/unpp/) It's 2008: Do You Know Where Your Talent Is? Why Acquisition and Retention Strategies Don't Work, p.6

These numbers reinforce the reality that the future global workforce will face not only an employee shortage but also a skills shortage. In dealing with that challenge, workforce planning initiatives must attend to four critical requisites:

- Recognize all four generations or "cohorts" in the workforce.

- Acknowledge that one-size-fits-all management is not going to work.

- Adopt a sense of urgency – opt for "speed now" and "elegance later."

- Create a "signature experience" for employees to improve their engagement.

Just what is a signature experience? Breakthrough research from thought leaders such as Tamara Erickson and Dr. Lynda Gratton indicate that it isn't enough for companies to say they are the best places to work and have great corporate culture. Companies that are really having success in the areas of talent attraction, retention and workforce planning are concentrating on three or four areas where they can claim bragging rights – the "signature experience," or "Hot Spots" as the researchers refer to it.

As a proof point for signature experiences, executives should look at *Fortune's* top ten companies list and review their innovative practices in talent management. These are the drivers that get them on that list. Leading-edge companies are focusing on creating signature experiences in areas such as hiring, employee development, recognition, total rewards and talent promotion.

A specific example of a signature experience that many organizations are using effectively is the use of storytelling, or actively promoting a unique perspective of the enterprise's history and values and the commitment of its people. It's a process that drives engagement and growth. It is also a test of truth as the storytelling needs to be truly reflective of reality or its sincerity will be mocked.

When it comes to managing the multiple generations of employees, internal and external workforce planning is the emerging priority. Companies that focus on it can stay ahead of the worker shortages. C-tier executives who don't take this issue seriously are putting themselves and their organizations at risk.

Right now there are sectors in the U.S. economy that are running short of qualified workers. Health care is facing critical shortages of nurses and radiologists, and the energy sector already has a shortage of engineering talent. Survival of an enterprise will be contingent upon attracting talent from a diminishing pool of qualified workers.

Exacerbating the situation, younger workers – those from the generations commonly known as Gen X and Gen Y – don't identify themselves through their work to the same extent as their elders, categorized as Traditionalists and Baby Boomers. While older employees often work long hours and see their work as a fundamental part of who they are, younger ones tend to have no desire to define themselves primarily through their jobs.

Boomer parents often are acutely aware that their own children have chosen careers that allow a better balance between work and life. Gen X and Gen Y employees are not lazy; they simply have a different set of priorities than their parents when it comes to work. Or as Tom Casey's children, Gordon and Amy, stated over a recent dinner… "Why should working for the family mean never seeing the family?"

Gen Y workers will enter professions like investment banking and consulting that have typically demanded total commitment and long hours. But even the monetary rewards that enticed people into such fields are probably not enough to get those in Gen Y to sign over their lives. The Gen Y hires want to do a good job for their employers, but work isn't all they want to do.

To accommodate the four generations, companies need to implement the following critical steps: 1) Ensure flexibility; 2) Offer educational opportunities for as long as an employee is working; 3) Create those signature experiences to attract and retain talented workers; 4) Differentiate rewards based upon performance; 5) Truly collaborate on issues big and small; and 6) Re-recruit employees every day.

It is imperative that organizations adapt to the new workplace attitudes about the role of work. Indeed, executives increasingly have been paying attention. Over the last three years we have been surveying executives on what issues they believe demand their immediate con-centration. Their awareness of the changing nature of their workforce is evident. Among their top responses:

- **Increasing employee engagement.** Studies before the economic crisis indicated that the percentage of highly-committed workers globally was 14 percent. In the United States, it was 21 percent. It is reasonable to assume those numbers fell, given the global crisis.

- **Leveraging social networks.** Very few CEOs surf Facebook or LinkedIn, but they know they exist and are powerful. To some, the word *Twitter* means a quiet laugh. Yet they want to know what can be done to leverage those tools to promote their enterprises.

- **Dealing with demographic shifts.** The C-suite executives are very aware of how the demographic shift is affecting their markets. This is a dramatic change from earlier attitudes. They also need a greater awareness of how those changes are influencing aspirations within their own enterprises.

- **Developing innovative pay practices.** The old ways just will not work. For example, it will be hard to motivate Generation Y employees with an Incentive Stock Option Plan. They do not plan their careers with a five-year "vesting" horizon.

- **Improving employee retention.** Recent Harvard Business School research indicated that approximately 20 percent of those whom organizations designated as "high potentials" chose to leave their jobs for roles at other organizations. That should send the message that the problem of engagement, which had been deteriorating before the crisis, will only be further complicated by shifting demographics and the anticipated post recession growth in employment opportunity. As indicated if HiPos leave even though they were in no danger of being the casualties of restructuring, they either a) did not know they were HiPos or b) didn't perceive the organization assigning material importance to the identification.

It would seem that executives who want their organizations to flourish have become ever more mindful of avoiding Einstein's definition of insanity: "Continuing to do the same things in anticipation of a different result."

CHAPTER ONE

Challenges of Talent Readiness

Not long ago, a poll conducted by the Society for Human Resource Management found that 70 percent of those in human resources were not worried about staffing challenges related to an aging and retiring workforce. In the years since, in the wake of the recent recession, executives have begun to realize the folly of this type of "head in the sand" attitude toward demographics and other key concerns.

They are coming to understand that they should be focusing on critical areas such as learning, career development, total rewards, talent acquisition and workforce planning. Those five components will drive engagement and determine their Talent Readiness.

The following graph illustrates our concept of Talent Readiness.

Talent Readiness – Getting It Right

GLOBAL TALENT READINESS

To achieve Global Talent Readiness it is necessary to have the Right **People**, in the Right **Positions** at the Right **Time** with the Right **Skills Sets** and the Right **Motivation**, derived from the Right **Mix of Employees, Vendors, Suppliers** and **Contingent Workforce Incumbents.**

Getting it right requires
**LEADERSHIP,
CREATIVE PLANNING** and
**INNOVATIVE HUMAN
CAPITAL PRACTICES**

THE THREE L'S OF TALENT READINESS

"Right people, right place, right time, right motivation" is the basic formula for Talent Readiness, and it involves many complexities, from shifting global demographics to the role of rapidly evolving technology. Yet the business case boils down to Three L's – leadership, leverage and legacy.

Leadership

Inevitably, all eyes and ears will turn to you, the leader, for answers. As President Harry Truman put it, "The buck stops here." But as a colleague of mine once said: "As a leader, you will often be called upon to demonstrate leadership when you feel least ready to provide it."

Leaders play an urgent role in safeguarding an organization's future. This can mean everything from helping capable managers effectively execute leadership roles to shaping succession plans.

Of particular importance in the leadership pipeline is Generation X, the smallest of the three predominant age groups in the global workforce. The bulk of that segment – mid-30s to early 40s – is the traditional feeder pool for leadership positions. Yet that same segment is the only age group that will shrink in the coming decade. The leadership pipeline very well could yield only a trickle. That demographic phenomenon is one key reason that executives need to model effective leadership as well as extend a helping hand to show this next generation the way.

Leverage

Leadership means many things. When it comes to Talent Readiness, it means finding ways to increase the capabilities and influence of those in the organizational chart. If you doubt the strategic importance of leaders' leveraging the abilities of those who work for them, consider the following:

- A survey conducted by Adecco Group North America showed that slightly more than *three-quarters* of employees questioned were not satisfied with career growth opportunities at their companies.

- Recent research by Bersin & Associates reveals that nearly 40 percent of line managers do not feel they have the training and skills to effectively manage employee performance. Yet when companies have highly effective talent management strategies, their average revenue per employees is 26 percent higher, Bersin's research shows.

In short, what leaders need to do is what their people want them to do: Help them grow. When leaders make talent development a key strategic priority – when they personally invest in developing the talent around them – they build organizational capabilities and leverage the full potential of their human capital. This raises an important question: Do your leaders have what they need to help others grow?

Legacy

Leaders who commit to self-development as well as to the growth of their people make an investment that yields a long-lasting dividend: a legacy. Developing tomorrow's talent is a job that must begin today. If Baby Boomers delayed retiring because of the recession, the silver lining was that they had more time to engage their younger colleagues, transfer their knowledge, and groom successors. Creating a legacy is not a one-shot deal that happens only at the time of retirement. A legacy can also be built throughout the milestones and transitions of a career, for instance by leaving a team or a department in better shape than it was when you started leading it.

There are no substitutes for the hard work and commitment necessary for passing knowledge and expertise from one generation of leaders to the next. There are no quick fixes, no silver bullets. To appreciate what's at stake, consider the following:

- In an era rife with downsizing, research has found that 30 percent of companies retain knowledge poorly or not at all when workers depart.

- A study by the Sloan Center on Aging and Work at Boston College showed that after the recent recession, employee engagement decreased among Generation X and Y employees – yet hardly changed at all for employees in their 50s and 60s.

■ In her book, "Retire Retirement," Tamara Erickson says that Baby Boomers' idealism will motivate many of them to make a positive difference in the later chapters of their careers – which can include leaving a legacy in one's organization.

In her farewell column for *Newsweek*, "Stepping Aside," Anna Quindlen may have said it best: "John F. Kennedy [said] that the torch had been passed to a new generation. But torches don't really get passed very much because people love to hold on to them."

Are your leaders holding on to their torches, or preparing to pass them? Is your next generation ready to pick up the torches? Following the Three L's of Talent Readiness will help you do right by your leaders, your employees, and ultimately your organization.

COPING WITH THE TALENT SHORTFALL

In the years ahead, as it becomes increasingly difficult to recruit and retain talented employees, executives must focus on the following five strategies as they adapt to trends identified in **Discussion Partner Collaborative** research.

1. Companies will need to retain and develop the talents of older workers. As the worldwide workforce ages, most developed countries are finding that employees over age 55 make up the fastest-growing segment. Yet most talent acquisition and development processes target younger workers, ages 22 to 40.

2. Companies must take great care not to appear to take their employees for granted. Worldwide, only 14 percent of employees would state they are highly committed to their companies – and our research indicates engagement levels slipped further during the recession. Can any company sustain its business and grow under such conditions?

3. Companies must renew their commitment to talent development – this, in fact, is a core expectation of their Gen Y employees. Leaders will need to be actively involved in the education of their employees. Our leaders from the Baby Boomer and older Gen X groups have developed themselves, for the most part, but Gen Y employees will find that intolerable. Yet in recessionary times, training is usually the first expense to be cut.

4. Companies will need to find better ways to motivate their workers. Existing efforts are insufficient, to put it generously, considering the emerging demographics. The demands of the new workforce will compel modifications to human resources services. Consider these findings from our research:

    a. Workers no longer just aspire to economic recognition for high performance. They demand it.

    b. Healthcare insurance is a dominant desire for all employees.

    c. Employees of all ages desire flexible time arrangements.

d. It is questionable whether Gen Y workers care about long-term incentives, given their tenure expectations at the outset.

5. Companies need to clearly establish their corporate culture. Without careful foresight and planning, an enterprise risks failing to advance its values and strategic mission. Over the decades, much has been written about the importance of culture, yet the ability to truly influence it remains elusive.

FEWER PROSPECTS FOR CRITICAL POSITIONS

Unless organizations can deal effectively with these factors, workforce shortages for some critical positions will continue and worsen. And don't expect higher than desired unemployment levels to mitigate the situation.

While the unemployment picture fluctuates, as an example in the U.S., data from the Bureau of Labor and Statistics show that several occupations may have too few workers to satisfy current demand, with the unemployment rate for those positions falling below 4 percent. That's the level that commonly is considered to be "full employment," when everyone who wishes to work is employed.

While full employment doesn't sound like a problem during a recession, the reality is that several industries, such as electric utility, mining, and oil and gas extraction, have been growing. A shortage of workers for critical positions would likely have a significant financial impact on an expanding company, and today's business leaders must have the competencies to attract and retain them.

Below are four groups of critical positions with unemployment rates below 4 percent. Three groups represent industries. The fourth identifies critical positions within Information Technology. IT is a functional department that arguably is the first corporate area severely impacted by demographic trends.

Electric Utility

Nuclear Engineers 0.0%

Nuclear Technicians 0.0%

Power Plant Managers 1.3%

Mining

Maintenance, Heavy Equip. 0.0%

Mining & Geological Engineers 0.0%

Roof Bolters 0.0%

Oil & Gas Extraction

Civil Engineers 3.0%

Maintenance, Heavy Equip. 0.0%

Petroleum Engineers 0.0%

IT Department

IT Engineers 3.3%

IT Hardware Engineers 3.5%

IT Managers 3.0%

FOCUS ON: IT - The First Wave of The Perfect Storm

Workforce planning has been a core initiative in Information Technology (IT) for some time, but for the most part hiring needs have been determined by a formula of growth and departures. Despite such lack of sophistication, however, many companies held back from making drastic cuts in their IT workforces in the latest recession. Staff reductions during previous downturns left them scrambling for key skills once the recovery arrived.

Having prudently managed this downturn, IT executives are also being careful about their hiring as the economy improves. Any staff additions will likely focus on critical skills – those that are either in demand or scarce, such as enterprise architects, project managers, networking staff and application engineers. Workforce plans are designed to help organizations recruit, develop and retain such sought-after skills. But even though most IT executives are receiving passing marks on their talent management execution, it is not because of a mature workforce planning capability. Creating a meaningful workforce plan remains a challenge for most. In fact, recent Gartner research indicates that only 30 to 40 percent of companies have a formal workforce plan in place, and the majority only plan ahead 12 to 18 months, using a formulaic approach.

This rudimentary approach to workforce planning is about to become useless. The labor market "perfect storm," combined with an emerging demand for global business and technology innovation skills, means that the human capital market we know is about to radically change. So, while the current workforce planning activities have been sufficient for a deep talent pool with relatively low turnover, they are grossly insufficient for the future market. With highly-skilled positions needed, the talent market will have a shallow pool with rising turnover. The CareerBuilder 2010 Job Forecast, a survey of more than 2,700 HR managers in U.S. companies of diverse sizes and industries, revealed that many companies are already feeling this talent pinch. Many surveyed said they would like to rehire strong players they let go during the recession, and some are planning to offer key employees increased compensation and benefits rather than lose them to retirement.

In this environment, talent concerns will need to shift toward retaining and engaging critical-skill workers who are pivotal for meeting operating metrics like sales volume, customer experience, and operating efficiency. For success in this type of environment, executives will require a robust workforce planning capability that can hold an organization in good stead through a three-to-five-year forecast of supply and demand for critical IT skills. The focus will need to be on maximizing scarce talent resources to meet rigorous marketplace demands.

◇◇◇◇◇◇◇◇◇◇◇◇◇◇◇◇◇◇◇◇◇◇

What can employers do if they face a shortage of critical position workers? Three things:

- **Understand the risk exposure:** Determine the severity by conducting an internal and external workforce assessment along five risk categories: supply, age, retirement, turnover and generational friction.

- **Prepare for a mindset change:** Change how you think about your workforce. Instead of viewing it as a homogenous labor pool, segment the workers who are in critical positions in a similar fashion as marketers segment consumers. Determine which workforce segments represent growth, attraction and retention challenges.

- **Look for nuggets:** Collect and share through storytelling success stories in which your organization and others are successfully attracting and retaining critical position workers.

TOP TEN MANAGEMENT CHALLENGES
FOR THE NEW WORKFORCE

As identified through **Discussion Partner Collaborative** research, here are the top ten challenges that management faces in dealing with the new workforce.

1. **Replenishing and deploying workers.** For many companies, attracting and retaining enough skilled employees will be a daunting task. A recent case in point was Essar Group, a global conglomerate that grew from 20,000 to 60,000

employees in three years; 55 percent of its workers had less than two years of tenure.

2. **Dealing with four generations.** For the first time, four distinct age groups coexist within an enterprise. In dealing with them, one size cannot fit all. For example, the Gap clothing retailer recently had 157,000 employees, the vast majority of whom were Gen Y, yet their leaders were predominately Gen X and Boomers. To be successful, the Gap must address the needs of its customer and employee base simultaneously.

3. **Maintaining a leadership pipeline.** Some organizations have the attitude that, "If cream does not rise to the top on its own, we will buy more cream." That is unworkable in the new talent marketplace. It's self-defeating for an organization to abdicate its responsibility to develop leadership in favor of allowing it to be self-directed.

4. **Defining competencies for success.** Our research suggests that in the new talent marketplace, we should take a fresh look at the leadership competencies that we assess and develop. Among the qualities needed are a truly global orientation, with cultural awareness and language abilities; an ability to identify the "next big trend;" and a desire to collaborate and persuade rather than rely on the "follow me" model.

5. **Preserving institutional memory.** The retirement of older workers, the Traditionalists and the Baby Boomers, will cause an increasing loss of institutional memory, which already

has slipped due to recessionary restructuring. Institutional memory — the collective experiences and knowledge of an organization — needs to be passed on to successors. Nonetheless, most enterprises lack the discipline and inclination to use the tools available to them for preserving it.

6. **Rethinking rewards and incentives**. Organizations need to rethink their formulas for plotting compensation, monetary or otherwise. They need to recognize that Gen Y is not interested in long-term incentive five-year vesting; that high performers can feel marginalized when their recognition is similar to that of lesser performers; that it is insulting to tolerate salary compression with the hope that it will be "secret;" and that there are some who would gladly forgo money in favor of generous health care or a flexible work schedule.

7. **Retaining Baby Boomers.** The undeniable truth is that there are more Boomers than Gen Xers. Practices that think of an employee at age 55, or even 65, as on the downward side of the employment curve are ignoring demographic realities — and the many advantages in retaining those workers. Tamara Erickson's research in this area indicates that though companies are aware of progressive ways to preserve that talent, their willingness to do so does not rise much above happy talk.

8. **Attracting and retaining Gen Y employees.** The point of view that "given time, they will think just like me" has its limitations. Our consultants' experience suggests a more

appropriate approach is to create respectful, motivating, and flexible programs that embrace Gen Y's differences. The research shows many companies are adopting such innovative methods.

9. **Improving employee engagement.** This is of paramount importance in the emerging talent marketplace and has been made even more difficult during recessionary times. Our research suggests what appears to be lacking is awareness of the differences in aspirations and motivations. Even sadder, our research indicates that there is a perceived lack of respect for an employee as an individual in many companies. If that situation doesn't improve, employees will find new opportunities and adopt an attitude that says: "It is not that I am not working, or not working hard, it is that I am not working for you."

10. **Redefining "work" and "worker."** The emerging talent marketplace will soon move beyond job descriptions, career stages and alternative sourcing. The definitions of work and worker will be reinvented. We believe the new model will access talent as needed – Talent Capability on Demand – with the support of collaborative tools and technology. The Internet allows access to the world at large and opens new strategies for using employees, contractors, vendors, and people with particular skills and talents, including retirees.

HOPE FOR THE DISPLACED

In 1973, a 23-year-old serviceman, oldest of seven children, was discharged from the military and sent home when his father died. A college graduate, he searched for a job to help his family, but the U.S. economy was in a recession – a bad one.

He tried newspaper ads, employment firms, the Veterans Administration, and his various networks and friends. He looked for six months, feeling frustrated and powerless. He concluded that one of the worst of human conditions was wanting and needing to work and not being able to do so. Ultimately he found a job.

Many victims of the recent economic downtown have had to deal with similar circumstances. They found their plight even more difficult to understand because greed, stupidity and carelessness caused the recession, as was well-documented in the media. There are many stories about how people have coped, but the reality of unemployment is daunting, and their spirits often flag.

Even in an improving economy, victory remains further down the road for many. Their quiet suffering is very real. Recent studies have indicated that those "above a certain age, with general management skills, from certain sectors" will remain unemployed for at least six months and, when they do find work, will likely be underemployed for an extended period. As they navigate to the next stop on their professional journey, they need time to recognize the skills they will need for success and to adapt.

The displaced are likely to find that success as they redefine how their talents can fit into the new workforce and as companies take a fresh look at the types of skills and abilities they need to recruit and retain employees. The development of Talent Readiness offers hope for companies and employees alike.

CHAPTER TWO

Investing in Today's Talent

The late-night TV debacle involving Jay Leno and Conan O'Brien is a good illustration of the Baby Boomer/ Generation X divide – and a cautionary tale for organizations seeking to harness talent across the generations.

As you likely know, O'Brien was the late-night NBC comic with an edgy, ironic sense of humor, characteristic of Gen X. Born in the 1960s and 70s, Xers were steeped in punk rock and new wave music during their teen years. Many saw their working parents caught in waves of layoffs in corporate America during the 1980s and 90s, one factor that shaped their detached, wary stance toward large organizations.

But O'Brien toed the line with network colossus NBC. After 11 years hosting *Late Night with Conan O'Brien*, he renewed his contract. O'Brien agreed to stay with NBC and take over *The Tonight Show* when host Jay Leno stepped down.

Leno is one of the more famous members of the Baby Boomer generation – those who came of age during the rebellious 1960s, paid their dues in the working world, and grabbed for the brass rings in their fields. Leno snared the ultimate late-night TV prize when NBC selected him to host *The Tonight Show* upon Johnny Carson's retirement in 1992. Leno reportedly won out over rival David Letterman because NBC executives thought Leno was more of a "company man" who would relate well with the network affiliate TV stations.

When Leno yielded *The Tonight Show* host chair, he began hosting *The Jay Leno Show*, a prime-time program that aired weeknights on NBC. Alas, both O'Brien and Leno's shows produced weak ratings. NBC's proposed solution? Offer Leno a half-hour show at 11:30 p.m. and push O'Brien's *Tonight Show* back to midnight. O'Brien was given two options: Accept the new time slot or leave.

He left – with a payout in the tens of millions of dollars – and Leno had his *Tonight Show* seat back. How and why this all came to be has been a matter of heated debate.

Seen through the generational lens, was Leno a Boomer who couldn't relinquish the spotlight? Could he not pass the late-night TV torch to his younger counterpart, as Carson had done with Leno nearly 20 years earlier? Or was Leno a valued network player seeking to rescue NBC's late-night ratings?

Was O'Brien a loyal corporate soldier who got burned – or a savvy, free agent Gen Xer who turned lemons into eight-figure lemonade? O'Brien appeared to be staying true to his Gen X roots. He chose a cable channel for his next late-night talk show because it offered him the most flexibility, autonomy and control. The agreement provided for O'Brien to own the TV show, with the cable network airing it.

What are the lessons here? Does your organization provide Boomer employees a graceful off-ramp to new roles where they can contribute and remain relevant? Do you help them pass the torch to the next generation and feel good about it?

Are you rewarding your Gen Xers for their loyalty? Do you meet them in the middle by providing autonomy, flexibility and opportunity to demonstrate ownership of the business in an entrepreneurial vein?

In the generational dialogue, your organization has a choice: Write your own witty punch lines – or be the butt of jokes.

MANAGING A FOUR-GENERATION WORKFORCE

Effective workforce planning strategies will require a shift in thinking from the "aging workforce" to the "multi-generational workforce," says Shelly Schmocker, Vice President of Global Talent Management at StepStone, the international online employment portal. Companies are stepping back and looking more holistically at how to develop programs and deploy technology that will speak to four distinct generations in the workforce.

Each age group requires a different approach when designing career and compensation strategies, motivating performance, and addressing learning styles. The biggest challenge, however, is encouraging collaboration among these four generations of cohorts. Each seems to be looking at the others, wondering, "What are they thinking?"

The Emerging Global Employee Values

Traditionalist	Boomer	Generation X	Generation Y
• Conformity • Stability • Upward mobility • Security • Economic success	• Personal and social expression • Idealism • Health and wellness • Youth	• Free agency and independence • Street-smarts • Friendship • Cynicism	• Hope about future • Collaboration • Social activism • Tolerance for diversity • Family centricity
Born 1928-1945	Born 1946-1964/5	Born 1965/6-1976-80	Born 1980-2000

Source: Based in part on "Meeting the Challenges of Tomorrow's Workplace," CEO Magazine, 2005

Among the four groups – Traditionalists, Baby Boomers, Gen X, and Gen Y – the largest numbers of workers are from Gen Y, even more than the number of Boomers. But just as we no longer can restrict our thinking to the aging workforce, we also cannot just consider how we can please Gen Y.

Instead, we need to answer the following question: "How do we best manage four active generations of workforce cohorts with differing expectations?" Employers understand the background and experiences that shaped Traditionalists, Boomers, and even Gen X. But they are still trying to figure out the expectations of Gen Y, and they may need to keep working on this for some time.

Baby Boomers' views of their Gen Y colleagues include some of the following generalizations:

■ Gen Y's don't have loyalty to the company.

■ They have poor communication skills.

■ They are impatient and don't respect authority.

■ They spend too much time online.

■ I can't get them to want my job someday.

Likewise, there are as many generalized perceptions about Boomers that are held by Gen Y workers, including:

■ They are inefficient.

■ They don't respect me.

■ They assume that I'm interested in the career path that "they" have chosen for me.

■ They are obsessed with face time and have too many meetings.

■ They don't give me the latest technology, and they don't use technology effectively.

The real issue that underlies generational stereotypes is a lack of communication. The breakdown in communication happens in both directions, and it leaves each party feeling frustrated.

To illustrate the difference between Boomers and Gen Y, consider an interesting tactic that some recruiters have used with success in hiring young workers – some see it as their recruitment "DaVinci Code." Gen Y tends to be very family-centric, and one way to win these young workers over is to involve their family in the hiring process. However, some employers are finding that they've hired the whole family. It is not uncommon to hear stories of parents calling employers to find out why their son or daughter got a poor performance review. Obviously, few Boomers can relate to that experience. In fact, a poll of Boomers found that about 60 percent felt that they would have been better off without parents at all.

Any company that thinks it can manage the expectations of four cohorts using a homogenous model is in for a shock. It is time to embrace a more flexible approach that is sensitive to each cohort. Traditionalist workers are going to be around for awhile, and Boomers for quite awhile longer. A multi-generational workforce exists now, and companies must think about the four groups and their expectations in order to keep them in the workforce and productive.

If a company isn't struggling now to get good people, it will be. The C-suite can no longer get by with happy talk in response to human capital management. The old approach simply will not work with such generational diversity in the workforce. Innovation is essential!

◇◇◇◇◇◇◇◇◇◇◇◇◇◇◇◇

CASE IN POINT: TOTAL REWARDS AND GEN Y

Dude, Where's My Money?

Tamara Erickson has written a number of books on generational differences and has sensitized many to the contrasting aspirations among the four cohorts in the global workforce – the Traditionalists, Baby Boomers, Generation X and Generation Y.

Gen Y will be a managerial challenge for quite some time. To Boomers, effectively acting as mentors and managers of this group is exhausting. They ask "why" incessantly, and they take unction when they are not consulted by the C-suite on strategy.

At the risk of seeming pedestrian, let's follow the money: There are three emerging Gen Y attitudes in respect to total rewards:

1. *Don't hire anyone at my peer level, pay them more, and expect that I won't find out.*

2. *Pay me at a level commensurate with my performance and self-assessment of same.*

3. *Forget the stock that will vest in five years. I won't be here.*

Einstein's definition of insanity applies here. Many of the total-rewards approaches that are in force globally amount to "continuing to do the same things while anticipating a different result."

Many of our clients have learned that unless the total-rewards strategy is sensitive to the aspirations of this cohort, the compensation will be de-motivational. Moreover, if there is salary compression and/or a lack of differentiation, the employees will feel that the organization is dismissive or at best unaware of their aspirations.

The one-size-fits-all approach to total rewards is obsolete for improving employee engagement. It needs to be reinvented as soon as possible.

◇◇◇◇◇◇◇◇◇◇◇◇◇◇◇◇◇◇◇◇◇◇◇

UNDERSTANDING WHAT SHAPED EACH GENERATION

To understand the expectations of the four generations in the workplace, one must examine what shaped them.

- **Traditionalists**, born between 1928 and 1945, were raised in homogenous families and neighborhoods. This generation witnessed the rise of the white collar job and a strong commitment to higher education. Traditionalists have a respect for authority and place a lot of value in receiving financial rewards and having security. A good example of the focus on security needs can be seen in how important healthcare is to this generation.

- **Baby Boomers,** born between 1946 and 1964, and in the U.S. were shaped by the Vietnam War, the Civil Rights Movement, and the assassinations of Martin Luther King, John F. Kennedy, and Robert Kennedy. Globally the influence was The Cold War, decolonization, and democratic experimentation. Boomers are more suspicious of authority than their parents as a result of dynamics such as pervasive corruption and threats of nuclear holocaust. Boomers are competitive by nature, but they do show some commitment to making a better world.

- **Generation Xers** were born between 1964 and 1980 – the oldest are in their early 40s now. This generation saw the end of The Cold War and the fall of the Berlin Wall. They were the first to experience the high divorce rates of their parents, and most had some exposure to parents or relatives losing jobs to the recessions of the 1980s and 1990s. The growth of the Internet and global access to information created a generation that is information rich. Gen Xers ask: Where can I get the information? They are self-reliant and have clear tribal affiliations.

- **Generation Y**, born after 1980, is challenging traditional hiring and recruiting practices. This cohort is upbeat and optimistic despite having been exposed to routine violence in schools and terrorism, which put many of these young people in an almost constant state of vigilance. Exposure to technology became ubiquitous for this generation, and its comfort with technology is unprecedented. Raised in a pro-child environment, members of Gen Y listen to their parents and respect authority. They are pro-learning, spiritual by nature, socially conscious, and have high self-esteem. They like to be mentored by Boomers rather than peers, and while they respect older and more authoritarian role models, they do not have a high regard for organizations. They recognize that work is just one priority in life, not the priority.

Because of such diversity in background, each generation must be considered individually from the standpoint of career expectations, mobility, development and recruitment. To ignore the needs and wants of one group over another is a very risky practice. The key to managing different generations lies in understanding what drives their differences and leveraging unique characteristics to create win-wins for employees, their colleagues and their employer.

THE NEED FOR DIVERSITY, TRAINING AND EDUCATION

Related to this increasing generational diversity among coworkers is the diversity and educational achievement of the population at large.

Companies have been paying lip service for years to diversity in the workforce, but it is time to recognize its great importance. It is a reflection of dramatic changes in the population. For the first time in its history, the U.S. Presidential elections put a person of color in the Oval Office, and women rose prominently in the ranks of candidates. Globally woman holding senior governmental positions is now a matter of course.

As an example, though the number of college graduates in the United States is increasing, the percentage of graduates as compared to overall population has declined. Consider the following statistics:

- Currently between 25 and 30 percent of the U.S. population attains a college degree and the U.S. – which once led the global list for college degree attainment – now ranks 12th among developed countries.

- In the future, employers will want college graduates for two-thirds (66 percent) of all new jobs created.

It is not difficult to see the problem here for U.S. employers, a situation that is replicated globally. Not only will there be a shortfall in the number of college graduates to meet demands, but there is also going to be a severe shortage of graduates with requisite skills.

Developing countries such as India will also face shortages of skilled workers. The more specialized the skill set that is needed, the more difficult it will be for companies to attract workers with appropriate skills. Demographics, skills and education are all factors that will influence available labor and will have differing impacts by industry segment.

Companies already are feeling the ramifications of the skills shortfall. Leaders need to look at this issue directly and acknowledge that they will need to focus on education. No matter their size, companies will need to play a larger role in teaching skills to employees through training and development. They must get into the education business and doing this well will contribute immeasurably to the employee brand.

◇◇◇◇◇◇◇◇◇◇◇◇◇◇◇◇◇◇

FOCUS ON: CONTACT CENTERS

The last two decades have seen the acceptance of "offshoring," or the practice of establishing contact centers and outsourcing business processes to countries such as India, Ireland, Chile and the Philippines. India, the most prevalent offshoring destination, has aggressively trained people to meet the knowledge demand and worked to increase the country's number of college graduates, particularly engineers.

The original appeal of offshoring was that it allowed organizations to leverage the costs associated with a less expensive labor pool without sacrificing quality. For major companies, savings can total hundreds of millions of dollars a year.

Outsourcing appears to be here to stay, but increasingly the outsourced service may be "onshored" in the rural United States or Canada. This trend is being fueled by a multitude of factors: rising labor costs abroad, a desire by some organizations to maintain control over key data and intellectual property and advances in high-speed Internet service outside costly urban markets.

Among other factors, many companies have experienced customer service quality issues with offshore call centers and found that locating certain business processes many time zones away was more complex and less economical than anticipated. Delta Airlines and United Airlines are two prominent companies that in recent years stopped routing customer service calls to India and chose to handle them in the United States.

In addition, during the most recent recession, mounting political influence to keep jobs in the United States, combined with state and local tax incentives to corporations, has made onshoring a more attractive business solution.

Whether a company operates its own contact center or through a service provider, the reality is that customer service is as important as ever — and customer needs, like employee needs, vary across the four generations. The center needs a talent strategy that addresses the generations and promotes the customer experience you desire.

The contact center experience will need to evolve beyond live agents and Interactive Voice Response systems, particularly for Gen Y consumers — the largest consumer group in the United States. A 2010 study by Convergys Corp., "Bridging the Demographic Divide," revealed that 47 percent of Gen Y respondents would like to use social media for customer service, compared to 35 percent for Gen X and 20 percent for Boomers. Yet a 2010 benchmark study by DMG Consulting, a contact center market research and advisory firm, indicated that only 6.5 percent of contact centers supported social media. The study revealed that only 24 percent of contact centers planned to add support for social media by 2014.

Younger employees, who on balance are more technologically adept than their older counterparts, can help contact centers continue to evolve and meet increasing demands for customer service inter-actions provided via Web-enabled phones, other mobile devices, and social networking avenues such as Facebook and Twitter. In particular, Generation Y employees' strong preference for collabora-tive work styles could ensure that contact centers stay on the cutting edge or ahead of it.

In a weak economy, the need for good customer service only increases. Consumers are more careful with their disposable income, and tensions run high as people struggle to keep their jobs and companies strive to retain customers and market share. To meet the needs of this economy's customers, contact centers cannot simply hire people to fill seats and answer phones. The customers standards are rising.

What does this mean for contact center operations? It means attracting, developing and retaining Gen Y staff members; conducting succession planning to provide opportunities for Gen X staff members, the smallest generational segment and the traditional feeder pool for leadership; and putting a priority on retaining the knowledge of experienced Boomers as they near retirement. Ultimately, it means changing the corporate perception of the importance of contact center staff to customer service and business strategy.

◇◇◇◇◇◇◇◇◇◇◇◇◇◇◇◇◇◇◇◇◇

DEALING WITH A DECLINE IN COMMITMENT

In addition to a deficit of skilled, educated employees, companies are now dealing with the challenge of employee commitment. Statistics show that both male and female workers show a decline in the level of responsibility they want to take on in their careers.

Boomers joined the workforce with the expectation of getting more responsibility and moving up the career ladder. It was why they went to work. Attitudes about allegiance to work started to change with Gen X, and that change is even more dramatic now that Gen Y workers have entered the workforce. Taking on more responsibility is a huge issue for many Millennials; for them, flexibility is most important. They exhibit restlessness and a desire for mobility.

This section deals with the need to focus on the experiences that drive the Generational differences and the implications at least for the front line of contact centers.

There is also a need to reinforce this understanding with an appreciation as to the necessity for tolerance.

◇◇◇◇◇◇◇◇◇◇◇◇◇◇◇◇◇

CASE IN POINT: THE CONTRADICTION BETWEEN AGING AND CLUELESS

The Need to Embrace the Contribution of the Older Worker

A recent Wall Street Journal article spoke of the challenges the legal profession has in maintaining as Partners, those over a certain age. The article spoke of a Partner who still practices at 79, who was challenging in court the position of his firm that he was "too old" to fulfill the obligations of being a Partner.

The article went on to speak about his actual productivity (among the highest billing), scholarship (a regular contributor to legal journals and opinion pieces), and reputation as a mentor (younger Partners revere him as a mentor).

So, beyond age... why this dilemma? His legacy firm stipulates that it was being prudent and needs to have a "mandatory retirement age" to make way for "younger Partners".

So in the legal profession, as is the case in other sectors such as accounting, contribution is not a consideration......the main one is age! Hmmm

Vitality is not a function of years.....it is preparation, outlook, health, and intellectual curiosity.....

Speaking of which......

The Need to Understand the Mental Model of the Younger Worker

A recent survey at Beloit College of incoming freshman had some interesting results. When asked for example, "Who was Michelangelo"? The response was "a computer virus". I thought this was obtuse until it was explained to me that in fact there was a computer virus called Michelangelo.

As a Boomer I thought it would be interesting to create my own quiz and of course answered my own questions as if I was a Freshman (I Wish!)

1.	What was The Cold War?	One fought in the Arctic
2.	What was The Long March?	The first Marathon
3.	Who was Beethoven?	A Dog who starred in a couple of movies
4.	What was the Kitchen Debate?	An argument my parents had in the Kitchen
5.	What is the Palmer Method?	The swing of an old golfer
6.	What is a Fountain Pen?	A fountain in the shape of a Pen
7.	What is a Pop Tart?	OK this one would be timeless

So which is more compelling, the answers of the incoming Freshman or the fact as a Boomer I did not know there were "2 Michelangelos"?

And more importantly is this an issue of age, intellect, or exposure?

Reconciliation of the Apparent Contradiction

For insight I consulted blogs by Tammy Erickson (www.tammy-erickson.com) and my nephew Sean a former Army Captain currently in Grad School in Germany (http://seanmaybeheard.wordpress.com).

In reviewing their writings, the WSJ article, the Beloit study, and most importantly my pro-Sistine Chapel response, I was thinking.....maybe this "you lose it with age thing has some merit"!

NAAAHHHH!

*There are too many aspirations **all who work** have in common:*

1. *The desire to be respected*

2. *The desire to be recognized*

3. *The desire to be mentored*

4. *The desire to be challenged*

5. *The desire to be provided opportunity **regardless of age**!*

The disconnections we note and laugh about to the point of cohort mutual mocking, are not a function of age....there are more accurate explanations.

Having given this apparent contradiction some recent thought I have concluded it is an issue of understanding and tolerance.

Moreover as we will need the energies of all who wish to work to be effective whether we speak of societies or enterprises, we had best table the ridicule and focus on more understanding and tolerance.

Companies are concluding that the generation that lived to work is a thing of the past. Work and career flexibility is the new paradigm. It is non-negotiable for Gen Y, and as companies scramble to find sufficient workers with requisite skills, they will need to figure out just how much flexibility they can "burn in" to their organizations.

Companies are aware that young workers are not going to work the kind of hours that older generations did. It is a struggle for some companies to even get Generation Y workers in the door, and companies are seeking ways to address the aspects of time.

It is widely acknowledged by most that it is not how much time you spend at work, but rather what you accomplish in that time that is most important. With their continuous connectivity, and the attitude that they can work anywhere at any time, Gen Y employees expect to work on their schedule, not yours.

◇◇◇◇◇◇◇◇◇◇◇◇◇◇◇◇◇◇◇◇

CASE IN POINT: EMPLOYEE ENGAGEMENT

During the recession, global enterprises did not distinguish themselves as encouraging their employees to be committed. One company informed its employees to call an 800 number before reporting to work on Monday to be told "if you have a job." Another company chose to displace some employees on Take Your Daughter to Work Day.

The ultimate insult was from a company whose human resources department issued this memorandum: "Don't be embarrassed sorting through your neighbor's garbage if there is something you need" – implying that it is acceptable to behave as if you are destitute if you are displaced.

Prior to the recession, Towers Watson did a global engagement study that indicated the level of those who perceived themselves to be "highly committed" was 14 percent. In the United States, it was 21 percent. Gallup found that employee engagement in the United States remained relatively stable during the recession. Boston College's Sloan Center on Aging & Work found that while engagement barely changed at all for Traditionalists and Baby Boomers, Generation X respondents reported decreased engagement, and Gen Y respondents reported the greatest decrease of all.

X and Y are not chromosomes. They are enlightened, intellectual, achievement-oriented, and self-confident employees. Discussion Partner Collaborative research shows they have similar aspirations: They want learning opportunities, career challenges, and differentiated compensation based on merit, and mentoring from qualified managers. They also want a progressive employer.

But all of those are mere noise if the enterprise breaks the social covenant. They will not tolerate insulting behavior directed at themselves and their colleagues. They are wired in, and they have the wherewithal to register their displeasure globally and powerfully.

◇◇◇◇◇◇◇◇◇◇◇◇◇◇◇◇◇◇◇◇◇◇

NEW RECRUITING STRATEGIES

How, then, are employers to meet the challenge of attracting and retaining Generation Y talent? The task is daunting, but it is a priority that cannot be ignored. The only reasonable way to figure out what Gen Y employees want is to engage them in helping to shape the company culture, work environment and compensation packages.

In the late 1990s, stock options were a perk offered by many companies to attract employees. However, to Gen Y, stock options are of very little interest. The vesting period is generally at least three years and more often five – an eternity for a Gen Y employee.

One thing is certain: Companies cannot hope to attract a new generation of employees without figuring out what drives their expectations. Recruiting them requires a new set of tactics than were previously used with success. Members of Gen Y are born consumers. Organizations need to market themselves to them. They need to speak directly to their expectations.

One employer that has had to change its recruiting strategy for Gen Y is the U.S. Army. The Army has continuously changed its recruiting message over the years to appeal to each new generation. The Army's message to Traditionalists focused on authority figures and encouraged Traditionalists to join the ranks of authority. A message of "Be All You Can Be" was marketed to the striving Boomer generation, while recruiting the Gen Xers focused on technology and collaboration while respecting uniqueness.

Today's Army, like other employers, has focused on the parents as a way to get the message to Gen Y. The overall message to parents is, "You've done a great job raising your children, so let us help you develop them even more." The key to marketing to Generation Y is to focus on its uniqueness, including communication strategies that speak directly to this age group.

The importance of managing the expectations of all cohorts in the workforce cannot be overemphasized. Generation Y employees will require a lot of energy from others within their organization, but they should not get all the attention.

The following table lists some of the steps that organizations should take to manage the expectations of Generation X and Boomer employees in the workforce.

GENERATION X	BOOMER
Help broaden their options – increase their sense of self-reliance	Encourage them to stay
Don't require moves that sever social connections	Create career options – including cyclic work
Give them control over their career paths	Offer them options for greater responsibility (as well as less)
Leverage their entrepreneurial instincts	Allow them to "win"
Provide family-friendly flexibility	Encourage giving back, through mentoring, community service, knowledge sharing
Invest in technology and provide the time to incorporate it	Provide opportunity (time and coaching) to experience new technology
Develop leadership skills	Leverage institutional memory
Seek out their views, and be prepared to hear they don't like the way Boomers have run things	Appointment as story tellers

Our hypothesis is that by addressing these differences we can create a learning laboratory for the best way to manage the expectations of Generation Y.

TAPPING INTO EMPLOYEE PASSION

Whether they are your seasoned Traditionalists or your Gen Y new hires, employees have the potential to be extremely passionate about what they do – and we need to tap into their passion and competitive spirit to get them jazzed again. By doing so, an organization can keep them engaged, committed and dedicated to the enterprise goals. A passionate employee who feels involved and appreciated is far less likely to take his or her talent elsewhere.

This shouldn't be a time of reactionary communication – employees want to understand the long-term view and see it played out as outlined. Think about what you want employees to remember about this time and frame your messaging and actions accordingly.

Following the steps to effective communication – announce, educate, adopt and sustain – you can help employees get up to speed on the current state of your organization as well as what's going to happen. Then you need to help them understand why certain decisions were made and how the business will proceed.

In spreading the word, consider whether you will go directly to employees or try to cascade the information. If going directly, try to build in a "heads up" for leaders/managers, perhaps a day before the information goes out more broadly, so that they have time to prepare and ask questions themselves.

Design your early communications around the business strategy and what's been done to manage the strategy, for example, including the purchase of the other brands. If such a move was announced but there was little follow-up to help employees understand the value to the business, they may now see these as negatives. Highlight how these businesses have done, and how they've contributed to the success of the company. If applicable, provide a global view.

Highlight media reports that might impact your business so employees understand what influences the success of the company. This helps your workforce understand the bigger picture and gives you a chance to explain that you have a strategy to manage through any economic climate.

Once employees are educated about the strategy – whether through regular meetings, intranet videos, social media or blogs – reinforce the message through your regular channels. Connect everything you can back to the strategy so employees really see that there is a plan in place and leaders are managing with that plan in mind. If something doesn't go as expected, help employees understand why and where it fits into the bigger picture. Remain transparent and share as much as you can about the business.

Reach out to employees to get their thoughts on initiatives, and recognize them for any ideas that are put into place. You will be helping your employees see that they have a stake in the business and showing them what they can do to advance it.

The goal is to get all employees, from each generation, to pull together as a team. You need to help your employees understand the business strategy and how the company is following that strategy. Then you want to refocus together on making the best product or providing the best service in your industry.

By doing so, you truly will be including your workforce in the success of your organization.

CHAPTER THREE

Strategies for Success

Investing in the talent of the next generation can mean the difference between business success – and failure. That's one conclusion from a new study of 2,500 publicly traded companies over a ten-year period that looked at changes in chief executive officers and returns to shareholders.

The Booz & Co. research revealed there was an average 2.1 percent rate of CEOs being fired for poor company financial performance in the short term. Even if a company was in the bottom tenth of performance over a two-year period, its CEO had less than a 6 percent probability of being shown the door.

The study said Boards of Directors might hesitate to replace underperforming CEOs in part because of a weak pipeline of candidates ready to take the helm. At the same time, more than 20 percent of companies go outside their walls to hire their CEO – despite the fact that these "outsiders" tend to underperform someone promoted internally to the top spot.

Our prediction is that once the dust has settled from the recession, there is likely to be more C-suite "churn" as boards review how the enterprise coped. This is substantiated by one of the review questions we are hearing right now from our clients: "I need a third party review of my performance in advance of a Board request." In fact, in mid-2010, global outplacement firm Challenger, Gray & Christmas reported seeing companies start to shift toward more growth-oriented CEOs, after sticking with their previous CEOs through the recession.

That Booz research echoes a conclusion of the book *Good to Great*, by Jim Collins. Of 11 top-performing companies studied over a 15-year period, only one was led by an outside CEO, meaning a person who took the lead role after being with the company less than a year. In addition, Collins' recent book, "Why They Fail," points out forcefully the downside of capriciousness in leadership changes.

The Booz study on CEO performance concluded there was ample room for improvement in board oversight, succession planning – and development of top leadership talent. **Discussion Partner Collaborative** research and client experience emphasize that robust development becomes increasingly important the higher an employee moves up the ladder. Unfortunately as an executive climbs the leadership ladder the developmental mantra is more likely to be "your on your own".

A Concours Group report, "Accelerating Executive Development," recommended that today's leaders take an active role in developing potential successors. The study urged companies to build executive development programs around the next generation of skills and competencies that will be demanded of leaders.

The next generation of C-suite talent awaits. They are the Generation X and Generation Y employees. Our recent research on younger employees documents that they expect ongoing learning opportunities and varied assignments to ensure their development and employability security. Most don't expect to have long tenures or executive suite roles in their current companies. Yet many are open to the prospect – if it seems possible in their organizations.

You can call it "organizational generativity" or just good business – but plan ahead for passing the reins of leadership to the next generation.

A WORKABLE WORKFORCE PLAN

The tragic truth is that most organizations' definition of workforce planning is a modest prediction of how many new people will be needed after attrition. Those who aspire to more elegance develop terrifically complicated plans complete with graphs, summaries, and dire predictions of calamity.

Instead, we suggest concentrating on creating plans that focus on "critical constituencies" – those enterprise roles that are the most essential and are not covered under senior level succession plans.

To determine who is or is not part of your critical constituency, focus on the employee's impact on profit and relevance to the development of new products. Then assess such issues as time to retirement, level of engagement, and relative salary.

The Critical Constituencies are those mission critical roles not encompassed in Succession Planning Process:

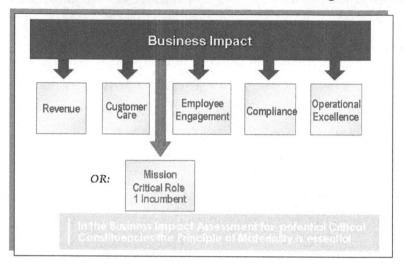

An external labor market assessment of these roles will determine the degree of difficulty in hiring. If you determine that the pool of applicants is extremely insufficient, consider an alternative sourcing strategy as part of the analysis. For example, instead of one full-time employee, an alternative scenario would be two retired part-time employees or contractors.

Through our research and client work, we anticipate that the ability to attract and retain qualified and skilled workers will only intensify. We therefore suggest that workforce planning endeavors focus initially on critical constituencies.

◇◇◇◇◇◇◇◇◇◇◇◇◇◇◇◇◇

CASE IN POINT: CRITICAL CONSITUENCIES

The Role of Critical Constituencies

In our pursuit of success, it is essential that we clearly identify the most critical roles in an enterprise and who are the most essential incumbents in those areas.

One of our clients is a large global insurance company. When the CEO was asked what the critical roles were in his company, he responded, "My direct reports." When we probed a little more aggressively, we determined that the most important role, or what we refer to as critical constituency, was, in fact, the actuaries.

When we met with the actuaries, we found that they felt disenfranchised and were "counting down the days." What was even more compelling was that the average age of this group was 59. As we would expect, actuaries understand retirement.

However, when we looked at the external marketplace, we discerned that the profession was not exactly a magnet for new recruits. Yet the actuaries were treated as if they starred in "The Revenge of the Nerds." They even had their own tables in the lunchroom.

When we informed our client that his most critical employees were nearing retirement, couldn't wait to leave, and felt badly treated, he did an outstanding job of recovering lost ground. Starting with an apology, he began focusing on initiatives such as flexibility to improve critical constituency engagement – operating by the adage that "sheer panic brings clarity of thought."

◇◇◇◇◇◇◇◇◇◇◇◇◇◇◇◇◇◇◇◇◇◇

Test your workforce planning IQ!

Below are some numbers, all of which are relevant to workforce planning. Think about these numbers before looking ahead to find the answers to what they represent. All of these numbers have recently been in the business press.

1. 24 percent, 18 percent, 11 percent, vs. about 10 percent

2. 55-65 years of age

3. 35-45 years of age

4. 39 percent decrease

5. One worker for every three retirees

6. Two for the family and one for the country

7. 20 percent by 2040

While you ponder those figures...

Let us position our point of view. Our client work has been influenced by shifting demographics and their implications for the emerging labor market. We frequently rely on research by Tamara Erickson. Based on this research, we believe that your competitive advantage depends upon elevating workforce planning to a core human capital process.

Now, the answers!

1. 24 percent, 18 percent, 11 percent, vs. about 10 percent is the difference between unemployment rates from the last century vs. the rate during the latest global recession.

2. 55-65 years of age is the fastest-growing segment of the U.S. workforce. This is at a time when most organizations perceive an incumbent at age 50 to be on the "back 9" of his or her career. It is becoming commonplace for professionals to take early retirement to work full time at a different company or to start a business.

3. 35-45 years of age is the part of the global workforce that is shrinking. This presents challenges for retention, career progression, retirement benefits, and development – to say nothing about hiring.

4. 39 percent decrease was in computer-science graduates before the recession. That obviously was influenced by the burst of the "tech bubble," but it indicates a domestic trend.

5. One worker for every three retirees is the prediction for Western Europe, which has a generous social benefit posture, for the most part unfunded – which will be a further restraint on the Euro Zone.

6. Two for the family and one for the country is an advertisement on Australian television that encourages larger families. The

shifting demographics have become a matter of national concern.

7. 20 percent by 2040. The increase is the prediction that to afford social benefits, Japan will have to encourage immigration, as the current percentage of non-Japanese working in the country is 2 percent.

Think about those numbers and what they mean to you and your organization. The statistics speak volumes. You may find them a not-so-gentle prod to placing immediate and high importance on planning your workforce.

ELEMENTS OF A NEW WORKFORCE PLAN

The core elements of a workforce plan focus on balancing internal predictions, strategies and cultural realities with the realities of the marketplace. To do so requires at least the following aspects in creating your plan:

- A comprehensive demographic plan. Develop scenarios based upon growth and global marketplace penetration factors.

- A breakdown of the workforce based on organization affiliation drivers vs. employee satisfaction – i.e., the same person who rates health care as good to excellent may not see it as a reason for feeling committed to the company.

- Employment flexibility (such as phase-down, part-time, virtual, etc.) without penalty in career progression, benefits, etc.

- A rethinking of leadership development and career progression systems. In China, 60 is a young age for someone on the fast track. In the United States, where the fastest-growing segment of the workforce is 55-65 and the second-fastest is over 65, it is time to challenge concepts of age.

- Development of an employee brand that can be taken seriously and does not prompt comments about lack of sincerity – for example, promoting your enterprise's concern for the environment.

In the following illustration, you can see our protocol for workforce planning. The need for effective planning has become self-evident, and so should a sense of urgency in accomplishing it. It is time to expand your definitions – and your horizons. The very future of your organization depends on it.

Assess Workforce Demographics / Develop Labor Force Predictions → Evaluate Critical Constituency → Identify Operating Model Improvement Opportunities → Build Transition Roadmap

LEADERSHIP EFFECTIVENESS

During the recession, **Discussion Partner Collaborative** consultants were often asked: "Do I have the right people to effectively navigate the crisis? After it has abated, will I have the right people to promote growth?" Unfortunately, our answer had to be "No!" The economic crisis brought out the best but also the less-than-attractive in many managers and organizations.

We have seen the following common denominators that inhibit progress:

- No objective mechanism realistically assesses and compares the proficiencies of managers. The assessment that "Peter is a good dude" may lack the necessary rigor to provide reassurance that you truly have the best.

- When the crisis started, virtually all developmental initiatives were postponed. The predicament this posture promotes is self-evident. How can you be assured of the best talent and skills when you are abrogating the need to invest in them?

- We have dropped back to the "new best friend" model, assertively hiring under the perception that "better people are now in the market, and we need to get them quickly." In our experience, we find this misplaced, and it has the unintended consequence of alienating your current employee base.

- The crisis has been at the expense of the proverbial good citizen. Every organization has them. These are the folks who really drive the enterprise but do not receive the accolades or perks of the high potentials. Be advised that with an improving economy and the continuing shift in demographics, this alienation will further hurt commitment.

So we must say "no" to leaders who ask if they have the right people in place when they have not attended to workforce planning. Well before the recession, there was a benign neglect for development, employee recognition and reward. It worsened during the recession, and sufficient planning still is not in place.

Now would be a good time to begin thinking of innovative practices that have been forsaken or that have barely received lip service. The crisis postponed but did not eliminate the impending challenges of talent shortfalls, nor of managing a differentiated demographic workforce. Whether we find ourselves in troubled times or improving ones, workforce planning is always essential.

◇◇◇◇◇◇◇◇◇◇◇◇◇◇◇◇◇◇◇

CASE IN POINT: PERFORMANCE MANAGEMENT

The Dilemma of Differentiation

A report in the Harvard Business Review focusing on Talent Management highlighted a Center for Creative Leadership study on high-potential employees. The findings showed the need to reconcile the fact that high performers are not always high potentials.

The article also indicated a need to ensure that assessment protocols or "rack and stack" approaches are based upon enterprise reality rather than a rigid application.

The following derived from a recent client experience:

A global financial services company had introduced a practice espoused by GE in which each year the "bottom 10 percent" was invited to leave the company. The selection of 10 percent was somewhat arbitrary, as those in GE would be first to acknowledge.

During the recession, many companies used many formulas to restructure. Those who are being brutally honest indicate that the recession allowed them to pare down the ranks "starting with those who should not be here." In a recession, such reductions increase productivity.

So we posed the question to our client: "Why are you continuing to arbitrarily take out 10 percent of your now-significantly *reduced workforce?" The client acknowledged that the 10 percent who would be leaving did in fact include some terrific performers.*

If you eat chocolate to excess, you'll get out of shape. And if you dismiss good performers to adhere to an arbitrary percentage set when times were different, you will reduce the enterprise IQ.

◇◇◇◇◇◇◇◇◇◇◇◇◇◇◇◇◇◇◇◇◇◇◇

TAKING THE INITIATIVE TO DEVELOP LEADERSHIP

Leadership is like love; it defies definition. And even those organizations that profess to do a good job in developing leadership acknowledge that there are issues that influence their success.

Most CEOs include among their stated goals a state-of-the-art leadership development process. As with many aspirations, the "process" can become dysfunctional despite the best of intentions of senior managers. The principal contributing factors are as follows:

- The CEO and top managers lack a visible commitment to the process.

- The process devolves into initiatives in search of a context.

- Clarity is lacking on strategy, linkages among programs, and benefits to managers.

- Cost factors frequently put process elements on hold.

- The program does not achieve performance or retention objectives.

- There is no mechanism in place to measure impact of the program on the business case.

Based on those considerations, my colleagues and I have begun experimenting with a concept we refer to as **"Inside-Out Leadership Development,"** focusing initially on critical constituencies. Although we support the development of competency-based development, performance management, and training programs, we have found that sustainable success in many respects relies upon first enhancing the skills of those most integral to the business case.

To that end we need to reduce our reliance on overly complicated competency models and assessment tools and construct our interventions around the answer to this question: What will it take to succeed in the organization in the future? There is an underlying theme in mind as well in that current performance does not necessarily predict future potential.

LEADERSHIP EFFECTIVENESS PROTOCOL (LEP)

Discussion Partner Collaboratives developed a methodology we refer to as the **Leadership Effectiveness Protocol** built around four levels of **Critical Success Factors (CSFs)**. Over the years, our experience using LEP has allowed us to predict general management competencies that define organizational success.

Our data are based upon more than 2,000 interviews of CEOs and their direct reports conducted since 1992. Our database includes companies from North and South America, Western Europe, Asia, and several Eastern European countries. The companies range in size from start-up through large multi-national. Our data also include interviews with senior executives from U.S. and foreign governmental agencies.

Future Leaders. CSFs Promote Integration of Endeavors

We have organized our findings into four categories: Threshold Attributes, Role-Driven Skills, Marketplace Differentiators, and Influence Management. In the creation of a truly effective leadership program, all elements must be considered.

- **Threshold Attributes.** Threshold Attributes are the "common denominator" skills required of all managers. These attributes must be possessed by all managers in abundance. A deficiency in one of them, in our experience, has to be corrected or we are not confident in predicting the manager's success.

- **Role-Driven Skills.** Success requires functioning as a specialist and thinking like a general manager. In a globally successful business, managers work together to define the company's place within the industry and its competitive posture.

- **Marketplace Differentiators.** Marketplace Differentiators are those skills possessed by an organization's managers that define its position in the marketplace. These skills involve promoting the organization's interests through strategic thinking and knowledge transfer. Together, these skills frame leadership and the strategic thrust of an organization.

- **Influence Management.** Organizations grow from the inside out. The influence skills of managers help to determine the organization's common sense of purpose. The crafting of an organization's culture, climate and social system is a consolidation of managerial willingness to push the enterprise's "levers" and face challenges to promote positive change.

LET'S TAKE A CLOSER LOOK AT EACH CATEGORY:

- **Threshold Attributes.** Successful general managers must be able to think strategically while acting globally. We have identified four common, indispensable skills:

  » **Global orientation:** As companies become more multinational, managers must be able to think in a "big picture" context and realistically assess the implications of their decisions on a multinational scale. Parochially focused managers are not traditionally successful, based on our experience.

» **Problem solving:** This is the ability to solve business-related problems creatively with a bias for action! Managers must have an aptitude to anticipate where difficulties are likely to arise and be able to address them innovatively before they worsen. Our data suggests that managers often encounter a bias against taking action and a lack of support for implementing "untested" solutions.

» **Communication:** Effective managers must be proficient in three styles of communication: one-on-one, in writing and through speeches and presentations. Internationally-oriented managers need to be culturally sensitive to the host country and speak the language.

» **Finance and Economics:** Successful managers, in our experience, have developed expertise in finance, political trends and international economics. All managers can read a profit and loss statement. However, most successful globally oriented managers have a "feel" for the broader international political and financial world.

■ **Role-Driven Skills.** Most successful general managers have gained a reputation as an expert in a specific discipline. There isn't one stairway to heaven: We have found successful managers to be champions of various critical business processes such as Supply Chain or Marketing. In our work outside the United States, two trends bear mentioning:

» Chief Financial Officers, traditionally considered to be logical successors, are no longer perceived that way so strongly. They have been supplanted by managers oriented toward Sales and Marketing.

» Successful international managers are proficient on the strategic use of total rewards, despite regulatory restrictions and inflationary conditions in the host country.

■ **Marketplace Differentiators** are the cornerstone of differentiation among managers. These skills define managerial potential and reputation within an organization. We have identified a number of proficiencies called External Leadership Attributes that we believe predict success for leaders:

» Strategic Focus. Successful managers promote successful companies. They understand the impact of their role on the business. Most importantly, they appreciate how their roles relate and depend upon the roles of others. They have the organizational and personal maturity to avoid internal rivalries; they realize that all need to be winners, or all will ultimately be losers.

» Leadership Style Alignment. We repeatedly observe that successful managers have more than one style they use with individual reports. Worldwide, when managers move up the career path, they increasingly delegate. Obviously, there is a need to do this based on demands of time. However, even in top positions, style ranges from directive to delegation, and they choose the appropriate style based on the proficiency and proactivity of their direct reports.

» Industry Knowledge. Successful managers have developed strongly held views on trends in their industry. Regardless of the amount of time spent in an industry, a manager should be perceived as having a strong knowledge about its dynamics and position in world markets. If a manager is coming from a different sector, extensive study is necessary.

» Integrity. Successful managers are role models in avoiding expediency. We have found that they refuse to compromise or cut corners, believing their personal reputation is at issue. These ladies and gentlemen epitomize management by values. The scandals at Enron, AIG and WorldCom, as well as the recent meltdown in the financial services sector, have highlighted this attribute. Independent of the Sarbanes-Oxley Act that attempted to raise ethical standards, these managers are the ethical standard.

» Stakeholder Relations. Mushroom management does not lead to success. The public, employees and stockholders need to know what's up. Successful managers have a flair for public relations – they write articles and op-ed pieces, give speeches and grant interviews. They also promote efficient communication within their organizations.

◇◇◇◇◇◇◇◇◇◇◇◇◇◇◇◇◇◇◇◇

CASE IN POINT: ETHICS

Ethics Isn't a Matter of Degree

You're on a 10 p.m. plane on your way to a critical presentation. You purchase a sandwich and proceed to drop it, staining your power suit, the one you had planned to wear in front of all those important people – clients and prospects who mean so much to your company's future.

When you arrive at your hotel, you find it offers emergency cleaning, but it costs $50. Your company does not pay for cleaning. How do you handle this?

1. You chalk it up to a bad day, and you assume the cost.

2. You write a feel-sorry-for-me letter to your employer and ask for reimbursement.

3. You get creative on your expense report.

We'd like to predict that most respondents would choose No. 1. But we would be wrong. More than 50 percent of respondents in a newspaper poll chose the third option.

So if we, as managers, are No. 3s, what message are we sending to the new generation of workers who, when disappointed, are not short on idealism nor militancy?

The above is a stark example, but consider one that is more benign: the lip service we pay to collaboration. When we espouse the tenets *of teamwork but behave in a contrary manner, those in Gen Y don't see us as shortsighted but rather as unethical. It's perceived as an unforgivable violation of trust.*

In this era of YouTube videos and the like, CEOs are coming to realize that when walking their own talk, they had better watch their step.

◇◇◇◇◇◇◇◇◇◇◇◇◇◇◇◇◇◇◇◇

■ Influence Management. Influence Management skills are the ones that show ability to make a difference within the organization's culture. These skills build internal trust in a manager as he or she progresses up the career ladder. The manager, through these proficiencies, becomes more accepted and credible when achieving a senior leadership position.

» Conflict Management. Successful managers make a good-faith effort to resolve conflict in a principled and fair manner. These managers engender a reputation for balancing assertiveness with compassion. Contentious issues are not allowed to fester.

» Network and Coalition Building. Successful managers are recognized for the quality of their relationships on multiple levels. Foremost are their internal and external networks. They are recognized as truthful. Effective team management and participation also predict success. This will increase in importance as the business horizon becomes more competitive.

» Staff Development. Everyone benefits when mentoring is positive. We have found that managers with reputations as sought-after mentors have predictably been more successful. Our proven hypothesis is that these managers have a better appreciation of the energies that can be harnessed through people. Most importantly, managers who are good mentors are usually good teachers. As they evolve to higher levels in the organization, building stronger relationships, they are more likely to have their visions followed than managers who are perceived as peevish and not having the time.

The Leadership Effectiveness Protocol has been for us a core consulting tool. Through this work, we have identified predictors for success. Our consolidated findings support our hypothesis that many of these skills cannot be taught. They require personal initiative to acquire.

Our hypothesis is not intended to diminish the value of organization-driven leadership development programs. We take the view, however, that organization initiatives - on their own, even when defined and managed - can only be relied upon to a degree. The managers themselves need to be participants in controlling their own destinies.

The talent in any company is its only appreciating asset. Therefore, putting developmental responsibility on the manager, as well as the organization, is a sensible proposition.

As you can see from the following graph, there is still much to be done at the enterprise level to significantly improve leadership effectiveness.

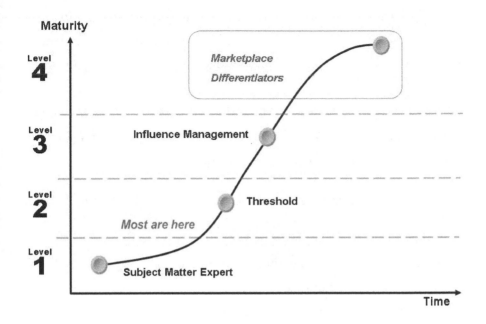

HIGH-PERFORMANCE EXECUTIVE TEAMS

Much has been written about why organizations need teams and why coalitions are difficult to achieve. Executives got to their rank by their individual performance and decisiveness. Working in teams wasn't what brought them recognition. Let's face it, folks: Eagles don't flock.

However, the need for teamwork is greatest during restructuring, when resources are rationed or absent – as evidenced by the words devoted to it in business periodicals and at countless meetings. Dr. Lynda Gratton has written several insightful books on this topic. She and Tamara Erickson published a seminal article in the *Harvard Business Review* on collaboration that highlights deficiencies in dealing with generational considerations – such as Gen Y, for which teamwork is an expectation.

To further complicate matters, some organizations, in their performance management and reward strategies, emphasize collaboration in spirit only. There is no tangible emphasis on recognition for participating in teams or leading them. Few organizations actually promote the need for teams, even if they say they do. They all maintain that cooperation is needed within and across departments, but few back up their statements with rewards or sanctions.

Just saying teamwork is a desired organizational attribute is a little like kissing your sister. A certain ambiance is missing.

My colleagues and I have been experimenting with various executive level team-building approaches as an extension or our organization and process redesign work. At the core is the need for highly proficient collaborative tools. Senior executives must acknowledge that developing the environment for high-performing teams goes beyond just framing the need and appointing the people.

Before interventions can build and sustain teamwork, we have found, the initial difficulty is in persuading executives that there is a true community of interests. They participate as spectators rather than in a meaningful, problem-solving way. They are usually sincere but often overly polite. They refrain from developing a workable coalition with a unique identity and tailored set of operating principles, and failure to do so creates a barrier to success.

Such was the case with a European company that after restructuring set up a Top Management Team with pan-European and American membership. One participant said of the TMT meetings: "We all retreated back to our nationalist borders and ignored the fact our very survival depended on each other." Commented another: "We all spoke English but listened in God-knows-what tongue." The popular excuse within the TMT was that cross-cultural differences were the barrier to success.

After a one hour speech on Effective Teaming Principles, we brainstormed on what was really going on in the company. Six hours later, after a workshop and debate, the managers emerged from the session having diagnosed the real problems as a lack of specific roles and the failure of the CEO to articulate the team's discretion in decision-making.

Frequently, major breakdown points are: 1) A lack of clarity on the purpose of the team; 2) Uncertainty whether the team is a decision-making entity or an adviser to the top manager; and 3) A lack of supporting technology, hindering communication because the team only can meet face to face.

Sometimes the basics are so simple they are overlooked. Each team must ask: "What is the question to which our formation is the answer?" Mission and charter statements do not go far enough. The team needs specific role delineations, identification of suitable topics to be brought to its agenda, and, most importantly, articulation by the top manager as to how he or she wishes to see decisions evolve.

Teamwork is disenfranchised at the executive level by what we call the "I am my function" phenomenon – that is, when people only represent the point of view associated with their designated role. For example, finance people only participate in financial discussions. This leaves much intellectual capital in the room untapped. The goal is to create an environment that affords an opportunity for members to demonstrate the broadest skills for the team's benefit.

STEPS TO BUILDING A HIGH-PERFORMING TEAM

Before executives can strengthen their potential for high-performing teams, they must recognize the limitations of the status quo. Our approach of "turning the mirror on the team" has a number of steps.

- **Organization climate diagnostic**: We have found that it is necessary to assess the organization climate to determine the convergence or divergence of views on factors such as the following:

  » **Role Architecture:** The clarity surrounding roles, accountabilities, reporting relationships and performance expectations.

  » **Performance Mentality:** The degree of organizational pressure to perform – meritocracy.

  » **Discretion:** The freedom, or lack thereof, of management discretion in decisions.

  » **Total Rewards:** The perspective regarding the competitiveness and generosity of the organization's compensation and benefits programs.

  » **Infrastructure:** The level of support from finance, human resources, information technology, marketing, etc.

  » **Commitment:** The level of perceived commitment to the organization for the next five years.

■ **Teaming workshop.** Our two-day workshops have three purposes:

» Creating awareness of the magnitude of barriers the team faces.

» Reaching agreement on role, meeting focus, decision-making discretion, and top management involvement.

» Developing a statement of operating principles, referred to as the Covenant.

■ **Developing a Covenant.** The teaming workshop process includes these elements, culminating in the development of the team's operating principles:

» *Examples of high-performing teams.* In the first step of our process, participants are broken into sub-groups and asked to give examples of high-performing teams. The five examples given most frequently are: sports (hockey or basketball), medical (ER or OR), music (symphonies), special operations (SWAT or Special Forces), and ants or bees.

» *Characteristics of high-performing teams.* Participants are then asked to identify those characteristics that distinguish high-performing teams. The most common attributes listed:

▫ Clear objectives, roles and accountabilities

- Tailored participation maximizing individual skills

- Tangible incentives for team performance

- Effective means of communication

- Conflict resolution procedures

- Sense of urgency focused on completion

Participants then compare desired characteristics with their own performance. The team is continually asked to assess the extent of any problems it sees and to develop action plans to reduce or eliminate barriers to success.

» *Organizational and personal awareness.* Using our climate diagnostic methodologies and the Meyers-Briggs personality assessment, we discuss how the team's work is affected by the corporate climate and the profiles of team members. We consider action plans to promote success. Meyers-Briggs is particularly useful in that the personality profiles point to diversity, which can be enhanced to promote group effectiveness.

» *Roles and protocols.* Working in subgroups, group members identify roles and decision-making protocol for the team. There is an emphasis on being specific.

» *The Covenant.* The program commonly culminates with subgroups developing "teaming principles." This Covenant becomes the contract by which the team conducts its affairs. After each subgroup presents its findings, the members of the team are asked, unless they have severe reservations, to initial the flipcharts or viewgraphs. We then display the Covenant, framed or as a table/wall setting, with signatures. We encourage the executive teams to communicate the Covenant throughout the firm – with obvious benefits.

YOUR COVENANT: ESSENTIAL ELEMENTS

In developing the Covenant that will govern how team members work together for the corporate good, numerous suggestions for operating principles will arise.

These are the most common ones:

- Everyone participates without exception.

- Do not let style and culture differences on the team become barriers.

- Listening is an art form, requiring care, thoughtfulness, and active involvement.

- Conflict is unavoidable, requiring principles for resolution.

- Assume good intentions; do not position people as accidents waiting to happen.

- Recognize that the overall interests of the organization are paramount.

- Communicate decisions consistently outside the group. No second-guessing or triangulation.

- Make the most of individual skills and contributions. No one fails.

- Whenever there is debate, make sure there is closure.

- Translate decisions into actions, with accountabilities and time frames.

- In evaluating group effectiveness, make use of metrics to show results, along with recognition and reward.

- Focus on high-profile and high-priority activities.

- Demand high-quality information for decision-making.

- To encourage wider staff development, allow people who are not members of the group to make presentations, participate in relevant discussions, and get a sense of the group's dynamics. Transform them into missionaries.

A lack of two abilities can sabotage the best of intentions and most disciplined agreements:

(1) listening skills, and (2) conflict resolution.

Executives' listening skills need to be tested and reinforced. Often, senior executives appear to be listening but really are thinking ahead about how they are going to respond – or, in many cases, about something totally outside the conversation. This must be confronted for the team to be most effective.

In human interaction, conflict will arise. No matter how much you wish to eliminate conflict, it will happen. Resolving it calls for principled communication and resolution, not finger-pointing. The group should agree in advance how it will handle these disagreements – for example, "The CEO makes the final call."

Organizing and maintaining high-performance teams takes energy – but the effort is worthwhile, both in the short term and the long. Your company's ability to grow and prosper depends on it. Self-interest must not be at the expense of what is good for the company. It's hard to captain your ship when members of your crew are counting their own fortunes rather than looking out for their mates.

To cultivate the talents of your employees, you need to enhance their skills in working as a team. You can strive to get the right people in the right place at the right time with the right skills, but you must also make sure they have the right motivation – to use their special talents collaboratively to help your enterprise grow.

CONCLUSION

Leveraging Your
Talent Readiness

As economic opportunities rebound, companies are seeking new and innovative ways to develop their most valuable asset – their talent. An *Economist* cover story highlighted the emerging global shortfall of skilled talent. Between 2010 and 2050, China, Japan, South Korea, Russia, Italy and Germany are among countries that will see their workforces shrink rather than grow. The fastest-growing segment of the U.S. workforce will be over age 55.

The realities of this situation are prevalent in many sectors of the economy, such as oil, utilities and health care as well as critical positions necessary in all organizations, such as information technology and qualified project managers. The implications are sobering for companies that are poised to explore new global markets.

The evolving corporate emphasis on talent development was documented in a recent study conducted by The Concours Group, which found that companies are initially focusing their primary attention on the top levels of the organization. It is not surprising, therefore, that many companies have reached out for professional assistance to help make sure their practices and initiatives are conducive to attracting and retaining those who will be their rising stars and core contributors. In the words of one of our CEO clients: "The old adage that 'necessity is the mother of invention' should be reworded to 'dread is a great driver.' "

THE GROWTH IN EXECUTIVE COACHING

When you hear the words "a growth of over 2,000 percent," your first hope may very well be, "I wish that was my portfolio!" Rather, this is the growth in the use of executive coaches since 1999.

During this same period, the overall corporate investment in executive development represented less than 1 percent of revenues. The explosive growth in executive coaching begins to make sense when you consider the current status of executive development in corporate organizations. Very recently, we have seen the introduction of executive coaching for core players who are essential to enterprise success but are not formally classified as high potentials.

Some like executive coaching because it seems exotic – like having a personal trainer. But it is also effective. The Corporate Leadership Council considers external coaching to be the single most effective developmental strategy for executives. Formal training was ranked fifth.

Our research has found five rationales for starting a coaching relationship to enhance an executive's skills and engagement. The four most common, in order, are 1) To groom "high potentials" for current and future roles; 2) To correct nonproductive behaviors; 3) To get advice on the caliber of a senior executive's leadership bench strength, and 4) To allow a senior executive to test an emerging strategy with a recognized subject matter expert, such as an academic or thought leader.

Another rationale for executive coaching is that it is fashionable. This does happen. Personally, we think buying a Hermes tie or scarf would be a less expensive solution if this is the driving justification.

As executive coaching has grown in importance as a developmental strategy, so have concerns about how to measure its impact. To ensure the success of the coaching relationship, in the experience of **DPC** consultants, a number of root causes of failure must be avoided. These include the following scenarios:

- A manager is informed that you need a coach without context or letting the manager participate in selecting the coach (although we stipulate that the final decision is that of the enterprise).

- The highest level of management is not involved in the coaching program nor apprised of progress.

- The relationship does not have predetermined criteria for success. The coaching devolves into sessions that are primarily focused on "How is it going?" This becomes a greater problem when the coach lacks the skills to confront the client when necessary or lacks the business acumen to have conversations in an appropriate context.

- There is no set timeframe for the relationship, which as a result can sometimes continue for an extended period regardless of the value delivered.

To optimize the executive coaching relationship, we recommend five steps:

1. Utilize coaching selectively and with those who will benefit the most – avoid the fashionable trap.

2. Allow the coaching client to be involved in the process, if not the selection of the coach. The comfort level will contribute immeasurably to the success of the initiative.

3. Set explicit expectations with the client and coach regarding desired outcomes and time frames.

4. Ensure that senior management is involved with the executive coaching program and its progress.

5. Do not have the same coach for executives who have any relationship with one another and/or organizational affiliation.

FINDING A COMPETENT COACH

In the spirit of truth in advertising, the notification of "Beware of Dog" should also apply to executive coaching.

The use of coaches is growing rapidly for two incongruent reasons. Foremost it has been well-documented that coaching is the most effective means of leadership development. Secondly, with the displacement of so many executives, there has been a proliferation of those who now carry the career title of executive coach.

The more cynical of us remember the late '90s, when a displaced executive was going to "start a dot.com." Today, that aspiration has been supplanted by well-intentioned but unprepared advisers calling themselves coaches.

It is doubtful one would feel comfortable being represented by a lawyer who hadn't been to law school, or being treated by a doctor who didn't attend medical school. So why should any executive feel sanguine about being advised by a coach who lacks credentials? The above is further complicated by the lack of any regulatory oversight of the "industry."

In a survey of clients, we asked: "What are the top five critical skills needed by an executive coach?" Here are the top five responses:

Strong business fundamentals. A coach needs to know enough about business to be credible with the client. Many coaches advise on strategy and operations, as well as on effective leadership or correcting some less-than-attractive behaviors. But in any capacity, effective coaching requires knowledge of what the client role encompasses and appreciation of its enterprise relevance.

Sensei tendencies. A coach should be able to weave in war stories and lessons learned from experience. We refer to such sharing of examples as "illustration advisory." Of course, a coach must avoid pontificating, as in constantly opining: "When I was a young manager...."

Willingness to confront. The desire to avoid offending to preserve economic security can be taken too far in a relationship. Sometimes you have to find a diplomatic way to articulate what amounts to "What the hell were you thinking?"

Intellectual curiosity. A client is entitled to expect that the advisor is staying current. Although the John Boudreaus, Noel Tichys, David Ulrichs, Jim Collinses and Michael Porters are in a class by themselves, coaches can enhance their reputations if they share insights from others and their own documented point of view.

Willingness to admit failure. Staying in a bad coaching relationship is like staying in a bad marriage. If it isn't working, the coach should be the one who initiates the separation of the relationship.

You will note that a competent executive coach is presumed to have a methodology and highly-attuned interactive skills. A coach's role is to offer a professional perspective, based on extensive experience and research, to companies striving to position themselves among the very best – and with the very best talent on staff. An executive coach can help a company find and develop the talent it needs to have the competitive advantage in an increasingly global marketplace.

WHERE NEXT? QUESTIONS TO PONDER

Our clients who are concerned about the Talent Readiness challenge often ask us to list the most important questions that leaders will need to answer as they look to a successful future in a rapidly-changing world. By getting an outside perspective and aligning it with their own insights about their organization, leaders can make informed and competent decisions that can leave a legacy for years to come. Based upon a blend of Concours Group and **Discussion Partner Collaborative** research initiatives here, then, are crucial questions to consider:

- **Do you know what your organization needs for its future success?** Do you know what specific organizational capabilities and individual skills will be required to support growth strategies, short and long-term? As with any good marketing or research function, do you systematically spend enough time looking outside for insights about what the future holds for your organization? Senior executives are well-positioned to gather insights as they work with sales, customer service, or HR relationship managers who monitor strategic external partners. It is also time to be more demanding of human resources, which is uniquely positioned to align such insights with what it knows about existing talent to help inform key business decisions. Do you know what talent investments your organization needs to make now to ensure its viability? Are you doing it before the competition identifies there is an issue?

- **What strategies do you have in place to address key talent gaps?** Do you have a workforce plan? Are you measuring and reporting progress to your executive committee and board? Have you determined which talent needs are critical to develop internally because they will influence your growth and which could be imported from other sources? Have you considered a broad range of options for talent investments? For example, consider whether your organization is making strides such as these: tapping into older adults for permanent or project assignments; recruiting younger workers more aggressively with attractive lifestyle-appropriate assignments; finding ways to rapidly onboard new employees or offshore existing employees; retraining to enable skills transitions; placing groups geographically based on "next generation hot spot" labor pool availability; replacing jobs or tasks with technology; and establishing relationships with industry network partners to supply technical talent or commodity-type services. Organizations must solve the flexibility issue to compete in this new world – flexible sourcing of talent, flexible work arrangements, flexible learning approaches and options, and flexible compensation and benefit solutions.

- **Do you have a culture that fits the future needs of the organization and the evolving workforce?** What shifts in the organizational culture do you need to start driving now? Besides written policies, are you aware of the unwritten rules? For our future success, we must pay attention to leader behavior now. Today's leaders may not be sufficiently attuned to the need to shift their own key behaviors if the organization is going to be competitive for finding and retaining diverse talent in this new world of work. Given that refining culture takes time, are you actively and consistently coaching senior leaders on how they need to rewrite the unwritten rules of the company?

- **How strong is your talent pipeline?** Has your leadership team identified the key positions influencing the current and future performance of the company? In what ways will the rapidly-evolving workforce demographics have the most impact on the talent pipeline for these critical positions? Have you adjusted your approach, from recruitment through assessment, development and retention, in recognition of those specific demographic changes? One of the most intriguing questions is how demographics will change the path to senior management. The current road to the top is long and arduous, especially for large global enterprises. Once there, increased shareholder pressure, tougher governmental rules, and rapid organizational change are causing significant turnover issues in the executive suite. To that equation, add the differences in aspirations and lifestyle preferences among younger employees, and you have the challenge of defining what it means to be a leader in the future. Will your talent pipeline be robust enough and your leadership development portfolio sufficient to yield the right number and type of talented senior leaders when the time comes?

- **How engaged is your workforce?** Have your employee surveys moved beyond worker satisfaction to the more provocative questions that determine engagement? How passionate are employees about the work they do, and how committed are they to your organization? Is the nature of the work personally fulfilling and worthwhile to the employee? In the competition for time and talent, employee engagement is an important part of the equation, and it differs for each cohort. Over the last several years, a number of companies have tapped into engaged employees for innovative ideas that increase customer satisfaction, driving the bottom line. What could be your touch points to influence a diverse workforce's impression of your company – and thus, its engagement?

- **In what ways have you created a culture of learning?** How will your company retain the institutional memory of those who are leaving? Are your employees equipped for their changing job demands? Employees of any demographic want to learn, though their needs, interests and learning styles differ. Traditional training centers will need to morph into sophisticated consortiums with expertise in a range of learning methodologies and technologies. They will develop your human capital and foster innovation. Companies at the forefront of this challenge are already growing institutional knowledge through social networks with a variety of technologies that appeal to different cohorts. Others are partnering with academic institutions to customize curriculums to recruit talented young employees trained "their way." With the new workforce, your culture of learning can be one competitive advantage. Are you ready to compete?

- **Is your human resources function able to face the workforce challenge?** Can HR broadly execute – effectively, efficiently, innovatively and flexibly? Are you global in your mindset, regardless of whether your organization is global? It is a wonderful time for those in Human Resources. The fundamental shifts in workforce demographics will change every aspect of what they provide for the organization. Human Resources professionals have an unprecedented opportunity to firmly establish themselves at the executive table and help the organization improve its decision making through its human capital.

In a recent survey of more than a hundred C-suite executives, **Discussion Partner Collaborative** asked them what they perceived to be the top ten important initiatives to address Talent Readiness. Here is what they told us they were looking for:

1. **Simplification of the "3 P's": Programs, Processes, and Practices.** There is a need to demystify human capital processes. Executives recognize that to be successful globally, agility will have to become a core competency.

2. **Support for global ambitions.** "All politics is local," Thomas P. "Tip" O'Neill, former Speaker of the House, once said. And we might say that "all business is global," though some executives idea of international sensitivity is enjoying Mexican food. This deficit in experience will have to be challenged.

3. **Leadership effectiveness.** As addressed in this book, senior leadership and human resources must lead the development effort, ensuing with the identification of critical constituencies and strategies for dealing with them.

4. **Social networking.** CEOs are only now beginning to appreciate the power of social networking. But most enterprises use it only modestly, such as for posting job openings. The opportunity for Talent Readiness differentiation in this domain is tremendous.

5. **Cost containment.** This now goes beyond negotiating better health-care rates. Companies must rationalize the cost of the human capital strategy. The task can be daunting, but it anticipates the trend of valuing "intangibles" for shareholder reporting.

6. **Thought leadership.** Executives who develop an established point of view on their sector and the world at large have an opportunity to distinguish their enterprise. They must recognize that the talent marketplace is becoming more competitive, with the confluence of social networking, green enterprises, and agile enterprises.

7. **Reinvention of Total Compensation.** Starting with pension and long-term incentive programs, total compensation must be recalibrated. This is in recognition of the departure of Traditionalists and Baby Boomers, the rise of Gen X and the emergence of Gen Y. The new workforce requires new offerings.

8. **Consulting model for Gens X and Y.** The research on the mentoring needs of Gen X and Y is unambiguous: Over 75 percent indicate that it is one of the most desired aspects in an enterprise. Over 60 percent indicate they would be willing to leave their job to follow a good mentor. This, in our opinion, compels a new "advisory" mentoring model: Mentors must act as personal consultants, approaching the relationship with a clear focus and measuring impact.

9. **Helping new hires become productive.** Once employees are hired, they will not necessarily arrive with a desire to commit to the organization. Generation Y workers are, by nature and ambition, mobile. Our research indicates that they will produce when they become assimilated and involved in a manner that enhances their aspirations. We recommend a

new metric, "Time to Productivity," to measure success in hiring and absorbing new talent.

10. **Impact of Talent Readiness.** Enterprises need to be able to measure the impact of Corporate Workforce Programs (CWP) improving their Talent Readiness. The authors perceive this aspiration to be the Talent Readiness Thirteen Commandments, or what we sacrilegiously refer to as Moses Plus 3. Our recommendations, as you can see on the chart, incorporate the need to 1) Measure the changes both for the enterprise and in its critical constituencies; 2) Set aspiration objectives; and 3) Evaluate the financial and quantitative impact of initiatives.

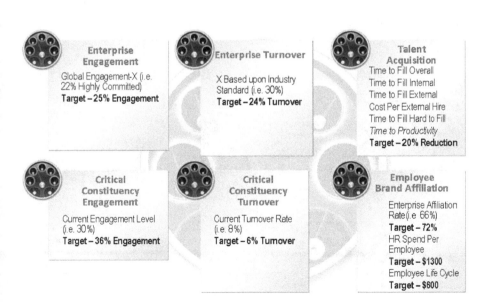

Enterprise Engagement
Global Engagement-X (i.e. 22% Highly Committed)
Target – 25% Engagement

Enterprise Turnover
X Based upon Industry Standard (i.e. 30%)
Target – 24% Turnover

Talent Acquisition
Time to Fill Overall
Time to Fill Internal
Time to Fill External
Cost Per External Hire
Time to Fill Hard to Fill
Time to Productivity
Target – 20% Reduction

Critical Constituency Engagement
Current Engagement Level (i.e. 30%)
Target – 36% Engagement

Critical Constituency Turnover
Current Turnover Rate (i.e. 8%)
Target – 6% Turnover

Employee Brand Affiliation
Enterprise Affiliation Rate (i.e. 66%)
Target – 72%
HR Spend Per Employee
Target – $1300
Employee Life Cycle
Target – $600

If an organization aspires to be more than a legend in its own mind, it must learn to effectively measure the impact of its Talent Readiness programs. Few enterprises have achieved this goal. Most enterprises are Level 1 in measuring maturity. The ultimate objective of a Talent Readiness strategy is to achieve Level 3 maturity.

Dr. Tom Davenport and Dr. John Boudreau, in their most recent books, agree there is a need to use metrics to truly assess whether a strategy is working. The table below lists what we believe to be some companies that are doing a better job than others. The Red Sox and Patriots are included not just because of the author's hometown loyalty, or to aggravate a New York-based contributor, but because both teams assertively use metrics in broad terms to determine athletic proficiency.

We would urge companies to avoid setting Level 3 as a short-term goal if they really have no programs in place. Rather, we would encourage them to tailor an approach similar to our "Thirteen Commandments."

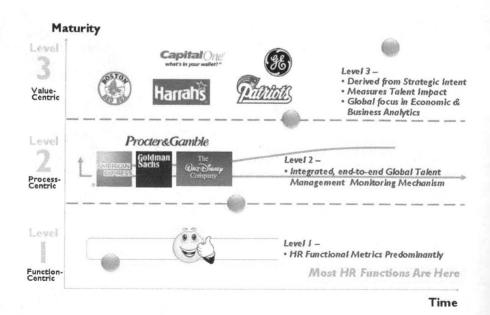

Talent Readiness is a journey best described in supply-and-demand terms. Essentially, it is this: What is the demand for enterprise sophistication? What is the supply of resources for innovation? In other words, what are the expectations, and what are your capabilities? By identifying these, you can achieve strategic alignment, rather than just having a portfolio of initiatives in search of a context.

Consider whether a Level 2 maturity is expected but you're only capable of Level 1. Or whether the company is in a start-up Level 1 mode – often the case in the biotech sector – and you can supply Level 2 programs.

These assertions and chart are heavily influenced by Dr. John Boudreau's work, in which he forcefully recommends that Talent Readiness initiatives should be measured in the context of a Decision Science, assessing both progress and impact.

DPC Talent Readiness Maturity

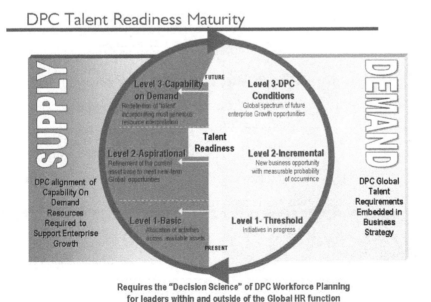

Requires the "Decision Science" of DPC Workforce Planning
for leaders within and outside of the Global HR function

CHARTING YOUR COURSE

For those who still feel buffeted by our Perfect Storm, it can seem hard enough just making it through till dawn, let alone stopping to listen to weather forecasts. But listen you must. With mounting financial pressures to perform, it can be hard to look outside your own organization and beyond the current year. However, the converging global workforce trends that this book has documented will demand that all of us think far ahead and well beyond our own boundaries.

Consider, again, the declining worldwide birth rate, longer life span, and the imminent retirement of hordes of Baby Boomers – to be replaced by new generations with far different career expectations. That is, if we can find those replacements – the talent shortfall threatens to hit us hard.

We are at a talent crossroads. We cannot follow Yogi Berra's advice that "when you come to a fork in the road, take it." We must be truly decisive, and now. We must objectively plan, innovatively create, and aggressively measure our initiatives for Talent Readiness.

It is critical that enterprise executives face the challenge immediately with inventive strategies. You need a vision of where you and your enterprise are headed and who will be the right people to get you there. This is necessary to stay competitive in a world of immense change. Foresight and action on Talent Readiness issues can ensure that a business strategy is translated into a bottom-line reality.

AUTHOR BIOGRAPHIES

Tom Casey, **Tim Donahue**, and **Eric Seubert** have worked together for over 10 years at PricewaterhouseCoopers, Buck Consultants, The Concours Group and now **Discussion Partner Collaborative**. Their blog is at http://talentreadiness.wordpress.com/

Tom Casey is the Managing Principal of **Discussion Partner Collaborative,** an executive advisory firm focused on Human Capital Strategy. An expert in the development of organizational transformation strategies during his 30+ years of consulting, he held senior positions with Harbridge House Inc., Arthur D. Little, PricewaterhouseCoopers, Buck Consultants and The Concours Group before founding **Discussion Partner Collaborative**. Tom has authored over 70 articles on Human Capital strategy. *Talent Readiness, The Future Is Now* is his third book on the topic. Tom resides both in suburban Boston and Lima, Peru "whichever is warmer at the time". Tom can be reached at tcasey@dpcadvisors.com.

Tim Donahue is Principal of **Talent Directions**, a New York-based consultancy specializing in talent advisory, leadership development and executive coaching. Before founding **Talent Directions**, Tim was with both PricewaterhouseCoopers and The Concours Group. Tim can be reached at timdonahue@talentdirections.com.

Eric Seubert is an executive advisor, author and platform speaker. He advises global clients on human capital transformation issues. Eric is a Managing Principal at **Talent Strategy Advisors**, a workforce planning and talent management consultancy offering advisory, executive education and insight research services. Eric's upcoming book *The Making of a Workforce Strategy* will be published in Winter 2010/2011 Eric may be contacted at eseubert@talentstrategyadvisors.com.

How can you use this book?

MOTIVATE

EDUCATE

THANK

INSPIRE

PROMOTE

CONNECT

Why have a custom version of *Talent Readiness*?

- Build personal bonds with customers, prospects, employees, donors, and key constituencies

- Develop a long-lasting reminder of your event, milestone, or celebration

- Provide a keepsake that inspires change in behavior and change in lives

- Deliver the ultimate "thank you" gift that remains on coffee tables and bookshelves

- Generate the "wow" factor

Books are thoughtful gifts that provide a genuine sentiment that other promotional items cannot express. They promote employee discussions and interaction, reinforce an event's meaning or location, and they make a lasting impression. Use your book to say "Thank You" and show people that you care.

Talent Readiness is available in bulk quantities and in customized versions at special discounts for corporate, institutional, and educational purposes. To learn more please contact our Special Sales team at:

1.866.775.1696 • sales@advantageww.com • wwwAdvantageSpecialSales.com

Printed in the USA
CPSIA information can be obtained
at www.ICGtesting.com
JSHW012041140824
68134JS00033B/3194